THE LITTLE GREEN GRAMMAR BOOK

MARK TREDINNICK—the author of *Almost Everything I Know, Bluewren Cantos, Fire Diary, The Blue Plateau*, and many other books—is a celebrated poet, essayist, and writing teacher. His bestselling books on the writing craft are used in schools and university writing programs and have inspired a generation of writers. His honours include the Montreal and Cardiff Poetry Prizes, The Blake and Newcastle Poetry Prizes, two Premiers' Literature Awards, the Calibre Essay Prize, and his landscape memoir *The Blue Plateau,* which was shortlisted for the Prime Minister's Prize. He travels and teaches widely and works with the corporate sector as a mentor, speaker and copywriter. The father of five, he lives and writes along the Wollondilly River, southwest of Sydney. He has taught creative writing, poetry, creative nonfiction, grammar and professional writing at the University of Sydney for over twenty years.

But even paradise must have rules. I do not know whether or not these rules were engendered in the beginning by divine deftness or by chance. I rather think chance was the origin . . . for the rules are neither nice nor neat; simply workable, and therefore, in the quest for life rather than no-life, sublime. Every vitality must have a mechanism that recommends it to existence.

—Mary Oliver, 'Flow'

THE LITTLE GREEN GRAMMAR BOOK

Mark Tredinnick

NEWSOUTH

A UNSW Press book

Published by
University of New South Wales Press Ltd
University of New South Wales
Sydney NSW 2052
AUSTRALIA
www.unswpress.com.au

First published 2008
10 9 8 7 6 5

National Library of Australia
Cataloguing-in-Publication entry

Author: Tredinnick, Mark.
Title: The little green grammar book/
Mark Tredinnick.
ISBN: 978 086840 919 1(pbk.)
Subjects: English language – Grammar.
Dewey Number: 428.2

Design Di Quick
Printed and bound by CPI Group (UK) Ltd, Croydon, CR0 4YY

CONTENTS

PROLOGUE—THE RULES FOR PARADISE

What grammar is and why you need it and how you master it 11

PART ONE—A NATURAL HISTORY OF THE SENTENCE

Sentence grammar, parts of speech, phrases, clauses and sentence types 19

1 The inner life of sentences 19
2 Who does what how 26
3 Word order 34
4 The declarative sentence and its moody friends 37
5 The sum of the parts 40
6 Communities of words—phrases and clauses 53
7 The families of phrase 56
8 The five canonical clauses 64
9 A brief history of dependency—dependent clauses and their uses 67
10 The four sentence structures 79

PART TWO—EVERYDAY METAMORPHOSES

Verbs, nouns and pronouns, and how they change shape; and a bit more about determiners 89

1 The taxonomy of verbs, nouns and pronouns 89
2 Verbs 91
3 Nouns 108

4 Pronouns 115
5 Determiners 125

PART THREE—KEEPING THE PIECES APART
The uses of punctuation *129*

1 'Trip 9s' 129
2 Different kinds of silence 131
3 The full stop (.) 133
4 The comma (,) 135
5 The colon (:) 150
6 The semicolon (;) 153
7 The dash (—) 159
8 The hyphen (-) 162
9 The apostrophe (') 173
10 The question mark (?) 179
11 The exclamation mark (!) 180
12 Quotation marks (' '; " ") 182
13 Brackets, parentheses, braces ([ ], ( ), { }) 191
14 The ellipsis (…) 195

PART FOUR—TWENTY-ONE GRAMMAR GAFFES AND HOW TO AVOID THEM
Common grammar problems and their solutions *199*

Introduction—Just between you and I 199
1 Dangling modifiers 200
2 Loose pronoun reference 202
3 Missing commas and hyphens 205
4 Starting a walk with *However* 207
5 Random and errant commas 209
6 Comma splices, fused and fragmented sentences 210
7 Subject-verb agreement 212
8 Fewer or less? 215
9 She and I or her and me? 216
10 Who or whom? 217
11 Me or myself? 218
12 He/she; he or she; or they? 220
13 Which or that? 224

14 It's or its? 226
15 Thomas's or Thomas'? 227
16 Bullet points and semicolons 229
17 Taller than I or taller than me? 230
18 Starting with *And*, *But* and *Because* 231
19 Ending with prepositions; splitting infinitives 232
20 Brian's conducting or Brian conducting? 232
21 Changing tense mid-sentence 234

EPILOGUE—LEARN THE RULES; FORGET THE RULES 237

References 243

Acknowledgments 247

Index 249

For Daniel,
who forgets some of the rules
and makes up the rest

PROLOGUE

THE RULES FOR PARADISE

WHAT GRAMMAR IS AND WHY YOU NEED IT AND HOW YOU MASTER IT

I

This is a writer's grammar. It's a grammar book *by* a writer *for* writers.

I don't want to put anyone off, but I'm neither a grammarian nor linguist; I'm just a writer who's thought a fair bit about grammar—and taught a fair bit of it, too. This book describes most of the grammar that's taught me how to write. I've written it down in case it helps you, too.

No matter what you write or hope to—novels, poems, papers, reports, articles, emails, blogs, letters to the council, policy, legislation, speeches, brochures, instructions, procedures manuals, wine labels or Christmas cards—you're going to need some grammar. This is a book of grammar for the writer in everyone. And I'm writing it because grammar counts. Grammar counts because it makes meaning possible, and meaning is what writers are trying to make. Or should be. Straight or circuitous; useful or artistic *meaning*. Grammar helps a writer make fast and economical—sometimes beautiful, sometimes shocking—sense.

So, in this book—responding to a need I rediscover on the news every night and in the paper every morning, not to mention in the letters from the council and the travel brochures and the strategic plans I'm asked to edit—I describe grammar the way I've come to understand it, the way I talk about it in class. This is how I make sense, for my own purposes, of the inner life of sentences; this is what helps me, now and then, write with grace, which is a thing grammar's good for.

By describing the way the language works and how it wants its sentences composed—the many templates, the few strict rules, the many irregularities and variations—I hope to help writers, from poets to policy wonks, move more sure-footedly through their sentences and paragraphs, their phrases and clauses and fragments. I hope to help them make the right choices by understanding better the beautiful, sometimes perverse, but mostly orderly and always generous system of the language—English—in which we conduct, many of us, our lives, and in which most of us, to some extent, make our livelihoods.

Grammar is the logic of the language. Grammar is the body of knowledge that allows you to master sentences and, making them more deftly and unambiguously, to say what you mean, neatly and memorably. For grammar starts and finishes, pretty much, with the sentence, that beautiful and robust tool for the manufacture of meaning. At very least, a good and meaningful sentence plays by the rules and therefore stands; it is a sentence—not something *resembling* a sentence. Unless it is a sentence, it cannot sing; it cannot make its unique semantic music. It cannot make great art and it cannot make much sense.

So, in this book, I'll be dealing with what really goes on inside a sentence.

- I'll define a sentence, in a way that should help you work out if you've got one there in front of you or not, and I'll talk about the many moods, modes, purposes and structures of sentence the language has conceived.
- I'll name the roles (the *dramatis personae*) on offer in a sentence (the subject, verb, object and modifier), whatever its shape.
- I'll catalogue the parts of speech (noun, verb, pronoun, adjective, adverb, preposition, conjunction, article and a few hybrids), and I'll explain their morphologies (how and why we spell them differ-

ently according to the use we put them to—in what tense, in what number, as agents or recipients of action, for instance).

- I'll describe the many species of phrase and clause a writer gets to trade with; I'll work through the uses of the fourteen (or is it fifteen?) marks of punctuation for which standard contemporary English has found a use (the way we score a piece of writing to make it sound the way we heard it in our head).
- I'll troubleshoot some common confusions, gaffes and debated or tricky usages.

II

There are schools of grammar, and I belong to none of them. Among the schools are traditional grammar, modern grammar and what is sometimes called *transformational-generative* grammar, the scientific-sounding grammar linguistics students learn these days. Rodney Huddleston of the University of Queensland is an undisputed leader in the field of contemporary linguistic grammar. I'm uneasy with the diction of this (dominant) school of grammar—it's hard going for a writer on deadline—and I'm uncomfortable with its claim to 'correct' the 'errors' of 'older traditional grammar'. But I can't fault its science, and throughout this book I refer often to Huddleston's book *A Student's Introduction to English Grammar*. No one interested in the ways and means of sentences can ignore it.

I'm more comfortable with the commonsense and plain-spokenness of modern grammar, whose queen is Pam Peters. Like her, I look at what the postmodern grammarians have to say, and I look back to the ancients, and I look in the middle, where Peters usually sits, in order to acknowledge disagreements and developments, to discuss differences of view, and in the end to come as close as I can to a clear and useful description of everything important. The larger part of grammar, I should say, isn't especially mysterious or contentious. But there are controversies, and there are areas where even now the scholars are trying to agree how best to make sense of usages that have been in the language since Chaucer's April showers. (How do we properly understand the infinite phrase, for instance, in *I'd love you to love me*? How should we characterise *to her* in *I gave my book to her*? And is it really apt to describe this sentence—*Take care of yourself*—as a clause in the imperative mood?)

The fact that grammarians still contend about the names and natures of such everyday usages shows how much like the rest of creation a sentence is, and how like a science grammar is (never finished looking for the best way to understand and articulate the world, in this case, of the sentence) and how language itself will always transcend our neatest conceptions of it. For grammar doesn't construct language; it describes the way it goes. Grammar tries to explain how language works, so that we might use language, especially on paper, with some insight and consistency, and in doing so keep it strong.

But I'm not a grammarian; I'm not a scientist of the language. I am, like you, a writer. And I've written this book so that I, like you, can spend more time writing and less time worrying about compliance. Over the years I've learned a few things about grammar. But you'd be surprised how many books I have open here on my desk as I write; you'd be surprised how often, in writing this book, I discovered how much more there was to understand than I had thought. The challenge isn't to know all the answers; it is to ask enough of the right questions.

III

Because grammar scares some of us witless, even though we practise it most of the moments of our waking lives, talking or writing; and because there's a school of thought that looks on grammar as a kind of tyranny imposed on our creativity by a cardigan-wearing cadre of joyless pedants, I offer you this metaphor for grammar. Grammar is the rules of democracy, which regulate and perpetuate this imperfect paradise of ours. It's the bundle of shared values, etiquettes, codified or inherited rights and obligations, along with a certain amount of governance infrastructure, all of which helps keep us in the freedom (of speech) to which we are accustomed. Grammar is, I suppose, that cluster of virtuous meaning-making habits. It is also the constitution that describes and proclaims them.

Now, as someone has said—with the activities of the CIA in mind—democracy can be overdone, and so can grammar. But we need some rules if we want what democracy allows us, if we want to prevent anarchy and tyranny. And we want some rules and we need to practise them if we want meaning to abound.

The rules of grammar are the rules for paradise.

The institutions and articles of democracy manufacture and conserve freedom. The rules of grammar manufacture and conserve language, with its power to make and share meaning. Grammar is the system inside the language; it is the constitution of the tongue. And if we want a community of sense—if we want to continue the vigorous and sometimes absurd and sometimes glorious conversation about ourselves and our world that we carry on in literature and government and everyday speech—then we'll need to know and observe our language's bill of rights: we'll need to learn and practise our grammar.

Now, I don't care for undue formality, the kind that pedantic insistence on grammar can foster. Grammar, like democracy, can be overdone. I like intelligent *informality*. We need a diversity of styles; each of us needs to find our unique voice and native syntax. That's the kind of democracy I'd fight for. I'm drawn, in particular, to the beauty of authentic vernacular, and some of that disobeys grammar. If you're writing, though, you'll need to obey more rules. Readers demand it; if they're to follow you without your waving arms and your twinkling eyes and the acts that accompany speech, readers need you to take more care with the words and how you lay them down. But you don't have to sound pompous. Good writers sound like good talkers—but a little tidier.

My point is this: getting your grammar down shouldn't make you sound like the Queen of England. Correctness doesn't entail formality. Sound sentences needn't sound stilted. Indeed, such writing will fail. It's a lapse of taste, a want of cool, no matter how correct it is.

So, relax your diction, but straighten your syntax. Stay cool; write like you speak, only better. The 'better' is where the grammar comes in.

IV

This book describes the system that is often called *standard* English. It looks at the structures of how we speak and write—and it describes and commends habits that have tended to help most writers and speakers make the most elegant and economical sense, nine times out of ten. It doesn't prescribe, or not too often; it describes, and it recommends, where a choice is open. Where I prescribe, I do it, I'd like to think, not for personal or pedantic reasons, but to defend the integrity and intelligence of the system—and the soundness of sentences generally. I do it to encourage writing that sounds like the best kind of talking—as vivid and humble, but more impeccably designed. I do it to help writers avoid embarrassment. I do it, if this doesn't sound too worthy, for the sake of the history and the future of the language.

I don't rail (too much) against breaches and abominations. And I don't speak against writing that stretches the rules—inventively, playfully, intelligently pushing sentences almost to breaking or pulling them austerely back. In fact, one wants such prose; we need as much of it as we can get. Let's all aim higher and take more risks and manufacture more beauty in our sentences. But anyone who wants to break the rules had better know what they are first. Ignorance of the law, they say, is no excuse for breaking it, and it won't keep you out of gaol (or is that 'jail' these days?).

'Learn the rules', wrote the zen poet Basho; 'and forget the rules'. Just don't ignore them. They'll set your writing free.

PART ONE

A NATURAL HISTORY OF THE SENTENCE

SENTENCE GRAMMAR, PARTS OF SPEECH, PHRASES, CLAUSES AND SENTENCE TYPES

1

The inner life of sentences

Many grammar books start with the parts; this one starts with the whole. We can come back for the pieces (the parts of speech, their names and behaviours) when we know what they're part of. When we know just what it is we fabricate with them.

What is a sentence; what does it do; how does its system work; what core relationships sustain it? This is where I begin. I start with deep structure—the thing a writer must master.

Every piece of writing, no matter how flat and useful, is a crowd of stories, and each of them is a sentence. Every sentence tells a tale: it names someone (or something) and tells you something about them—what they did; what they are; or what happened to them. What a sentence names is the subject; what the rest of the sentence tells you (about the subject) is its predicate.

Sentence by sentence, your reader looks for that short story. Good, sound sentences tell that story, and tell it clearly, no matter what else they do.

The other things good sentences do include linking themselves to other sentences forward and aft of them, illustrating their idea, complicating their initial simplicity, qualifying their points, and building rapport with their readers. But before any of that they must do their core business, which is to name that person or thing and tell you something sensible about them.

Stylish sentences, no matter how simple, no matter how complex, are strung on sound syntax. They make it clear who does what (and sometimes to whom); that is the through-line of any sentence; it's what the lawyers call the sine qua non—the thing we cannot do without.

Here are some:

1. Rain fell.
2. The river flooded.
3. Every sentence tells a tale.
4. My mother died on a fine Saturday morning in the month of August, in the year 2000.
5. I have a vision of an eloquent Australia.
6. She is a poet with an MBA; there aren't too many of those.
7. Never trust the artist. Trust the tale.
8. This chapter defines tax expenditures and describes their magnitude and scope.
9. We live in circumstances that are not of our own making.
10. An explosive document was tabled last night in Council.

Every good sentence contains a subject and a predicate. And within that predicate is a verb that's finite, a verb that's fixed in time. So, had I written

> Every good sentence *containing* a subject and a predicate

I would not have made a sound sentence. You notice it doesn't *sound* like one? It sounds like a nonfinite clause waiting for an independent clause to hang from. It's not fixed in time; *containing* is a present participle that just keeps going on and on. *Containing* would also be called a *verbal*. Verbals are incomplete and nonfinite verbs, which serve as either nouns (*writing*, *jumping*, *losing*) or modifiers (*broken* finger, *dripping* tap, *falling* market). A finite verb—which every predicate needs; which the central story requires—has *tense*, in other words. *Contains*, in the sentence I wrote, is expressed in the simple present tense, a tense that describes action that is happening now and tends always to happen. (For *containing* to be fixed in time, it would need the help of the verb *to be*, thus: *is containing* or *was containing* or *will be containing*. Which doesn't sound quite right because it implies that that action is located at, and proceeds from, a more specific moment than is the case. (I talk more about tenses in Part Two.)

In addition, a sound sentence must be *independent*. Every good sentence is complete; it wants nothing, grammatically speaking; and it has nothing added to it that strips it of its self-reliance. So, if I alter a couple of the sentences I gave you in the list of examples earlier, thus

> *When* the river flooded.
>
> *After* my mother died ...

neither would be independent anymore; the little words (prepositions) I've inserted at the head make them depend upon—make them subordinate to—another clause that never comes. They have become, by the addition of subordinating words (subordinating conjunctions), subordinate or dependent clauses. Each is now something less than a sentence. On it own, each would be called a sentence fragment, not a sentence.

Finally, the words in a sentence must follow conventional word order. English is fairly loose and generous about this, but clearly some word patterns produce a scrambled sentence, not merely an awkward one—if you get the words way out of recognisable patterns, you have not made a sentence:

> The never trust artist. Tale trust the.

(I say a little more about conventional word order shortly.)

Let's look more closely at each of my sentences, pointing to the subject and predicate, and explaining anything else that arises.

1 *Rain fell*. *Rain* is the thing this sentence names; *rain* is its subject. And what does the sentence say about the rain? That it *fell*. The predicate here is a finite verb, and that's all.

2 *The river flooded*. It's the same story with the river and its flooding, except that *river* has *the* in front of it. *The* and *a* are called *articles* or *determiners*. More on them later. *The* is adjectival, or modifying: it helps signal which river.

3 *Every sentence tells a story*. *Sentence* is your subject here; *every* modifies it (you'd call it a determiner too). All the other words are the predicate; among them, *tells* is the verb (in the present tense); *story*, the thing that gets told, the noun that receives the verb, is the *object* of the verb and of the sentence. Notice that it has the indefinite *article* (*a*) in front of it.

4 The opening sentence of Donald Antrim's 2003 essay, 'I Bought a Bed'—*My mother died on a fine Saturday morning in the month of August, in the year 2000*—contains this simple sentence (an independent clause): *My mother died*. *Mother*—plus the possessive form of the first person personal pronoun (*my*)—is the subject of that core sentence; *died* is the heart of the predicate, a finite verb (an intransitive verb that does not require (as *fell* and *flooded* did not, either) an object). One just dies; one doesn't die anyone or anything, though sometimes one dies adverbially—*beautifully* or *badly*, *painfully* or *quickly*. The rest of the sentence—the rest of the predicate, if you like—is four word clusters (phrases), one beginning with the preposition *in*, one beginning with the preposition *on*, one beginning with *of* and the last beginning with *in*. Each of these prepositional phrases tells one a little more about the main event—different aspects of *when* it happened.

5 *I have a vision of an eloquent Australia*. Subject: *I* (first person personal

pronoun). Predicate: *have a vision* and perhaps also the prepositional phrase that follows (*of an eloquent Australia*). *Of an eloquent Australia* characterises (modifies or describes) the nature of that vision. Within the predicate, the finite verb is *have*, and its object is the noun *vision*.

6 *She is a poet with an MBA; there aren't too many of those.* I've married two sentences with a semicolon, here. Let's take them one at a time. *She* is the subject of the first; the rest of the words compose the predicate; within them, the finite verb is *is*, and *a poet* is the subject complement. This is the first example so far of the structure of sentence that names something/someone and then tells you what she/it *is*. The verb *to be* (*is*, here; present tense and singular, because *she* is the subject) does not describe action performed by a subject and passing to an object. (*She loves a poet* uses a normal kind of verb, where the loving is performed, as it were, by the subject *she* upon the object *a poet*. *She is a poet* identifies the subject of the sentence and the noun that follows the verb. *What is she? A poet*.) *With an MBA* is a word cluster, specifically a prepositional phrase, and it tells us what kind of poet she is. You'd call this phrase a modifier. *There aren't too many of those* has the same structure. The subject is *there*; it's called *the existential there*. The verb is *are*, made negative by the addition of *not*; *too many* is the subject complement; *of those* is a modifying prepositional phrase.

7 Each of the sentences so far has been a declarative sentence. It tells you what something *does* or someone *is*. I was always told that each such sentence, like each sentence so far, was in the indicative mood. To call it a declarative sentence is to say the same thing, I've learned in more recent years. More on this later. I mention all this because D H Lawrence's epigram—*Never trust the artist. Trust the tale*—gives you two sentences in the imperative mood. Neither contains its subject; its subject is, if you are reading the sentence, *you*; that is, the reader. Although a legitimate sentence is meant to contain a subject, sentences like these, in the imperative mood, are regarded

as sentences, on the ground that the subject is always implied. So, the subject is the putative *you*; the predicate is *never trust the artist*; *never* modifies (negates) the verb (in the imperative mood) *trust*; *the artist* is the object of that verb. *Trust the tale* follows the same course, but positively.

8 *This chapter defines tax expenditures and describes their magnitude and scope.* Here's a simple sentence of some sophistication. It contains one subject—*chapter* plus its modifier *this*—and a predicate that includes two verbs, each performed by that same subject—the verbs are *defines* and *describes*. *Defines* is followed by its object, *tax expenditures*, and the second verb, *describes*, is followed by its *two* objects, *magnitude* and *scope*, the conjunction between them, and the modifier *their* in front of them.

9 *We live in circumstances that are not of our own making.* The subject is *we*; it's followed by the verb *live* (present simple, plural); and the rest of it is a modifying phrase, beginning *in*, which contains a subordinate clause (it's actually a restrictive relative clause) *that are not of our own making*, all of which characterises the nature of the living. The *that* clause serves the purpose of delaying, until after the noun *circumstances*, the concept *not of our own making* (*out of our control*, if you like), which characterises (indeed, it defines) that noun, those circumstances. I called the *that* clause a *clause*, because it has in it all you need to be a sentence (subject *that*, plus finite verb *are [not]*); so, it's more than a phrase, but less than a sentence, because its subject, by its very nature as a relative pronoun, subordinates the clause to the main clause (*We live in circumstances*).

10 *An explosive document was tabled last night in Council.* Here is a sentence that names something (*[an explosive] document*; the subject) and says *what happens to it*. This is a sentence in the passive voice. The predicate contains the verb *was tabled*, made up of the verb *to be* (*was*; singular, past tense) and a past tense form (the past participle) of the verb *to table* (*tabled*). When you write the verb this way it reverses

the normal flow of action. The subject does not perform the action expressed by the verb; it receives the action. In this sentence, as is often the case in the passive voice, we are not told who did the tabling—who is the agent of the action. The rest of the predicate is made of two modifying phrases, *last night* and *in Council*.

To summarise the story of the sentence so far …

A sentence names something and says something about it; a sentence is a subject and a predicate. The predicate will contain, at very least, a verb, and that verb will be finite—fixed in time. But there's one more quality a group of words needs to graduate as a sentence. A fully fledged sentence must have grammatical *independence*. *Independence* means that the subject–predicate combination is not subordinate to some other word group nearby. What might otherwise be read as a sentence falls short of being so read if it begins with a word or small group of words like *because*, *after*, *although*, *as a consequence*, *despite the fact that*; or because the subject or object of the clause in question is a relative pronoun—*which* or *that* or *who*—none or which will bear the weight of an independent sentence. There are some other reasons a clause may lack independence, but these will do for now.

> *Although she is a poet with an MBA* no longer has independence: it wants a main clause to explain and complete it.
>
> Similarly *Because we live in circumstances that are not of our own making*.
>
> And *That are not of our own making*, within that sentence, is dependent by virtue of the *that*.
>
> *Which was tabled last night in Council* (where I've replaced a noun phrase *an explosive document* with a relative pronoun) also now fails the independence test.
>
> And finally *I have a vision of an eloquent Australia* loses its status as a sentence if I stick *if* on the front:
>
> *If I have a vision of an eloquent Australia …*

2

Who does what how

Think of a sentence as a play. There are only four parts on offer. That's it. Once you learn those parts, there isn't a thing in a sentence you can't explain; there isn't a variety of sentence, long or short, comic or tragic, you cannot script or deconstruct.

So, here's the cast—the *dramatis personae*. The:

- subject
- verb
- object
- modifier.

Anything that isn't manifestly one of those is *part* of one of those—it's a phrase or a particle or an article, hanging off the costume of the subject or the object, pulling the strings of the verb or the modifier. Because that's all there are. There aren't any more. And they're what I'm going to talk about now.

In case you're sitting there trying to find the four parts in some of my sentences, or some of your own; in case you're thinking *it can't be as simple as* that, I should warn you that it takes a little practice. What makes it tricky sometimes is that each role can be played not only by a single word, but by a cluster of words—a phrase or a clause. Like this:

> I left my car on the street and walked over a few dozen stumble stones and rang the bell in the brick portico under a peaked roof. (Raymond Chandler)
>
> {I: *subject*} {left: *verb*} {my car: *object*} {on the street: *modifier*} {and: *a joining word*; okay, so I didn't mention them} {walked over: *phrasal verb*} {a few dozen stumble stones: *object*} {and: *joiner, again*} {rang: *verb*} {the bell: *object*} {in the brick portico: *modifier*} {under a peaked roof: *modifier*}.

I suppose I should have added that there might be more than one subject, verb, object and/or modifier on stage, as here, at any given time. There might be two or more leads, and two or more support actors, and two or more verbs and any number of modifiers, or none at all. And to be completely honest, there are a couple of other quasi-functions that I'll come to later: or at least there are a couple of fancy names for bit parts that occur often enough and closely resemble the main ones. I'm thinking of *appositives* and *complements*.

> Her baby was *a tiny mouse with huge ears*. (Kate DiCamillo) (Here, *a tiny mouse with huge ears* isn't the object of the verb and it certainly isn't the subject; it is the complement of the subject. It is what *her baby* is.)
>
> John, *the youngest of the three*, surrendered first. (*The youngest of the three* is neither a subject nor an object; it is an appositive to the subject. But you could get away with calling it a modifier.)

Looking at a sentence this way—focusing on the four functions within it, rather than hunting down and labelling its many individual pieces—exposes the logic of the thing, the structure on which its meaning is strung, or from which it's falling loose. *Functional grammar*, which is what some people call this approach, helps you make out and, in time, strengthen, the bones that make the body of your sentences stand or fall. It gives you a rapid X-ray of the skeleton of the thing. And they didn't tell me a thing about it when I was at school.

So the play is the thing, and here are the players—not just their names this time, but brief character sketches.

a *The subject* is the thing a sentence *names*. It may or may not be what the sentence is about—in other words, its *topic*. The subject, structurally, is the part of the sentence that one names in order, then, to say something about. If my sentence goes *It is raining*, then *rain* is my topic, but *it* is my subject (the *existential it*). Where the predicate says what the subject *does* or what it *is*, one can say that the subject *performs*—or carries out or enacts—the verb. In a passive sentence, the subject receives the action expressed by the verb. In general terms, to encompass these related but different functions, the grammar books say that the subject *operates* the verb. Find your verb; ask yourself which word (or word cluster) is driving it, being it or being driven by it; and you'll have found your subject.

> *The copperhead lay on the road in the sun. Lay* is your verb. Who lay? The copperhead. There's your subject.
>
> *The match is in the balance.* What *is*? The match is. *Match* is your subject.
>
> *The matter has been settled.* What *has been settled*? *The matter*; that's your subject.

b What, then, is the verb? *The verb* is the word (or group of words) that supplies the action—or other dynamic element—the sentence describes. The verb sets the other (static) elements (those things and their hangers-on) in motion; it makes them act; it lets them interact. It tells us what happens (*runs, loves, writes, loses, wins, makes, cries, dies, performs, enacts, decides, thinks*), or what is (*is, seems, means*). The verb is the *doing* or the *being* word.

c The *object* is at the receiving end of the verb (where the voice of the verb is active, that is). It is the word or phrase that receives the action expressed by the verb; it is the thing directly affected or produced by it.

> I love *you*.
>
> ASIC regulates *corporate behaviour.*
>
> You want *what I've got*.
>
> We manufacture *software*.
>
> Ideas Inc creates *advertising concepts* and sells *them* to clients.

What I have described so far is called the *direct object* of the verb. Grammar also recognises the *indirect object*. Again, it will be a word (a noun or pronoun) or word cluster that stands at the receiving end of the action expressed by the verb, but there will already be such a word or phrase in the sentence—the *direct* object. Indirect objects occur when the verb in question involves some element of transmitting something—giving a message to, taking lunch to, presenting the report to, and so on.

The indirect object receives the object that receives the verb (*you* receives the *it* that receives the description, in the sentence that follows):

> Let me describe it to you.

Picture this: a courier has a parcel for you; she pulls up at your place and puts it in your hands. If that scenario were a sentence, the *courier* would be its *subject*; *giving* would be its *verb*, since that is what goes on; the *parcel* would be its *direct object*, since it gets given; and *you* would be its *indirect object*, since you receive the object. You receive the object that receives the verb. Thus

> The courier gives *you* the parcel.

Or to put the same thing differently:

> The courier gives the parcel *to you*.

Here are a couple more examples of sentences involving direct and indirect objects.

> The Deputy Secretary couriered *him* the report. (*The report* is the direct object; *[to] him* is the indirect object)
>
> He brought lunch to her. (*Lunch* is the direct object; *[to] her* is the indirect object)

In the second example, the indirect object is expressed through a prepositional phrase *to her*. Generally, you can write it either way (*He brought her lunch* is the other way, but it's confusing because *her* could also be the possessive, which would make it read as *He brought her lunch with him*. The characterisation and function of each part of the clause remain the same. Indeed, the first example might have been phrased like the second and the second like the first, without a change of meaning. Some grammarians, including Huddleston, view *to her* as a prepositional phrase, and not an indirect object. But, as opposed to the examples I'll give you next, *to her*, though it looks like a prepositional phrase, performs the same function as *her* in *He brought her lunch*.

When, on the other hand, the sentence makes no sense if you write the *to him* or *to her* bit the other way, you really do have a prepositional phrase, and it really is a *modifier*.

> Today she delivered her maiden speech to parliament. (This can't really be *Today she delivered parliament her maiden speech*.)
>
> I made my complaint to the editors. (This can't be *I made the editors my complaint*.)
>
> She made love to him. This doesn't mean the same thing as *She made him love*.

d The *modifier* plays a supporting role; it's a word or word cluster that has something more to say about the whole sentence (when its action occurred, for instance; why it matters) or about the subject or the verb or the object.

> *This morning*, she's wearing a *purple* shirt.
>
> *Despite everything we've tried*, we *still* have a possum *in the ceiling*.

Not every sentence employs all these functions. Often a sentence goes without an object.

> Jesus wept.

Here you have just a subject (*Jesus*) and a verb (*wept*; the past tense of the verb *to weep*). There's no object and no modifier, either. And look at this one:

> Call me Ishmael. (Herman Melville)

This sentence contains no express *subject*. (It's implicitly *you*, because Melville's famous sentence is expressed in the imperative mood.) So, first comes the verb *call*; you have, then, its object *me* (accusative case of the (first person personal) pronoun *I*); you have, then, the proper noun *Ishmael*, which is performing the role of the *modifier* here. In this case it modifies the object *me*. Or *Ishmael* may be an appositive to *me*.

> I watch the children playing on the table.

Here, you have all four roles. Subject: *I*. Verb: *watch*. Object: *the children*. Modifier: *playing*. Second modifier (part, really, of the modifying phrase *playing on the table*): *on the table* (a preposition, *on*, and its object, *the table*). The modifying phrase, *playing on the table*, would be called *adjectival* because it modifies the noun *children*, the object of the sentence.

> Sitting in my study, I watch the children playing.

This is the flipside of the last sentence. It begins with a modifier (*sitting in my study*), then moves to the subject *I*; it moves on to the verb *watch*, and its object *children*; it closes with the word *playing*, a verb form (present participle) modifying the object *children*. Another way to explain the last bit of the sentence would be to say that the phrase *the children playing* forms the object of the verb. *Playing*, in any event, is an adjectival verb; it would be called, in some quarters, a *gerundive*.

> Hope is the thing with feathers. (Emily Dickinson)

Here an abstract noun, *hope*, is the subject; *is* is the verb. There is no object, because the verb *to be* does not take an object; it passes no action to any noun on the other side of it; so, instead, you get *the thing*, a second subject (or *subject complement*). And then you get, in Emily Dickinson's beautiful sentence (I've only given you the start of it) a closing modifier, the phrase *with feathers*. That prepositional phrase modifies *the thing*, making it an adjectival modifying phrase.

> At last I saw the house that Jack built.

At last is an opening modifier. *I* is the subject. *Saw* is the verb. *The house* is the object. And *that Jack built* is another modifier (a clause, this time; specifically, a restrictive relative clause). The word cluster *that Jack built* describes (indeed, again, it defines) the object of the sentence, *house*. (Within that clause, you have its subject, *Jack*; its verb, *built*; and its object, *that*.)

> On 13 February, the new government used the first sitting day of the new parliament to issue to the Stolen Generations a national apology, which it had promised, in opposition, to do.

Let's take this apart. Here you have a sentence, *The government used the first sitting day to issue an apology*, and a bunch of modifying words, phrases and clauses, all of which together flesh out the full meaning of the sentence. Indeed, a fair bit of what the sentence is about is expressed in the modifiers. *Government* is the subject; *used* is the verb; *[the first sitting] day* is the object.

To issue ... a national apology is a modifier in which the heart and real topic of the sentence are told; you'd call it an *infinitive phrase*, and it contains a verb (*to issue*) in the infinitive, an object (*an apology*) and a modifier (*national*). *On 13 February* is a modifying phrase; *new* is a modifying word; *of the new parliament* is a modifying phrase; and *to the Stolen Generations* is another, of some importance.

The words beginning *which* compose another modifier, this time a modifying clause (specifically a nonrestrictive relative clause), telling us something more about the character of the apology, or perhaps the act of issuing it on the first sitting day. It is a clause because it contains a subject (*it*) and a finite verb (*had promised*), plus the connected verb phrase, *to do*. *Which* is the object of the subordinate clause; *in opposition* is another modifying clause.

> All he ever wanted was to play for the St George Dragons.

This sentence links a subject with a subject complement, by means of the verb *to be* (*was*); but each of those two elements is a word cluster of some length. The subject is the clause *all he ever wanted*, and its subject complement is the phrase *to play for the St George Dragons* (an infinitive verb and a prepositional phrase).

> She cooks like an angel.

Here you have a subject (*she*), a verb (*cooks*) and a modifying phrase (*like an angel*).

> He is irascible.

Now, you have just a subject (*he*), a verb (*is*) and a single-word modifier, the adjective *irascible*.

And, finally, let's try one in the passive voice:

The leisure centre will be completed by December 2009.

Subject first; passive-voiced verb (*will be completed*) next; modifier last (*by December 2009*). There is no object in the sentence; there never is in the passive. Effectively, the subject takes on that role: it receives the verb. If the actual actor gets mentioned, it is in a modifying phrase like *by the developers*.

3
Word order

Sentences in modern standard English normally put the subject in front of the verb and the object after it: *subject—verb—object* is the template for the main clause of most sentences you'll want to write. (The modifier, as you see, goes wherever it chooses, to best modify whatever it modifies.)

You'd write *Reading can save your life*, not *Your life reading can save* (object, subject, verb), which sounds Yoda-esque and has a history in older English (as in *Your wife I shall be*), but not much place in contemporary conversation. If we use this order these days, it would be to emphasise the object or subject complement. This is the case in the wife example, or in *Cricket they liked more than any other sport*. Or one's boss might say: *Your future at the company, I mean*. One might write: *She spoke very well, I thought*. Other modern languages, such as Spanish, I think, if the post-match interviews with Rafael Nadal are any guide, favour the object–subject word order—*My backhand I struck it well all night*—and other word orders apply in other languages.

In these sentences, we recognise an unconventional and awkward word order. There's nothing strictly wrong with them; but they don't go the way orthodox sentences go. My very articulate German friend, hanging a new door for me, just explained:

> I came up a new idea with.

And here's a line from a poem awkwardly inverted to achieve a rhyme (with 'daily'):

> 'To say I love you' on the phone you sing gaily.

You grow up hearing your own language; its order comes naturally and sounds right to you. So, if English is your tongue and I gave you this scrambled set of words:

> ink on laptop lying table and pen a the see an you.

... after a little mucking about you'd probably come up with this:

> You see a laptop and an ink pen lying on the table.

Not

> A laptop and an ink pen you see lying on the table.

Of course, it could be

> Lying on the table, you see an ink pen and a laptop.

But this might suggest it's you lying on the table.

In the imperative mood—because, I suppose, the subject is omitted—one starts with the verb or sometimes a modifier, as Lawrence did in *Never trust the artist*.

> See the child. (Cormac McCarthy)
>
> Look at me.
>
> Stop!

Please submit your proposal by Friday.

In the last of these, *please* is a modifier, too; in this case it would be regarded as an adverb, meaning *if you please/if it pleases you*. Which makes it something much less than a command, much more like a request or a disguised question.

In *Gentlemen, start your engines*, the opening word *Gentlemen* is, of course, the real subject of the sentence—not because it is the thing named, but because the gentlemen are the entities implicated in the command, *start*. The subject, it is said, is implied in a directive sentence. Grammarians would say *Gentleman*, where it is included, as here, is used *vocatively*; that is, you address the gentlemen in question directly, rather than casting them as the subject of a declarative sentence. In other languages, such as Latin, one spells the vocative noun and also the imperative verb distinctively, to make the usage and meaning plain. You might recall this is the problem Brian runs into in *The Life of Brian*, when he's caught writing *Romans, go home* on the walls of the town square.

When your sentence is put as a question (making an interrogative kind of sentence), you often start with a verb (or part of a verb phrase) or, if you start with a pronoun or adverb or some such, you still put your verb (or part of it) ahead of your subject:

Did you get *what you were looking for?* (*Did get* is the verb phrase here; *you*, its subject, splits the two parts of the verb; *what*, the object, comes next.)

What are you looking for? (The subject *you*, splits the verb phrase *are looking for*. This time *what*, the object—of the verb phrase *are looking for*, or, put differently, of the preposition *for*—comes first.)

Are you looking *for this?* (Asked this way, you start with the verb *are*, the first part of the verb phrase; the subject *you* comes second.)

Whom do I give *this to?* (Indirect object first, then verb, then subject.)

Do I give *this to him?* (Verb, then subject, then verb, then object, then indirect object.)

May I come in? (Verb before subject, before verb + particle.)

Is it too late? (Verb before subject before subject modifier.)

In one structure of declarative sentence, you use a word order very like the question: *Only after we moved to the country, did we start to see the sky*.

4

The declarative sentence and its moody friends

When I was at school, sentences—strictly speaking, their verbs—had moods, though not as many as I did. Most grammarians now view *mood* as old technology: an outmoded characterisation of the purpose of a sentence, borrowed from Greek and Latin grammars and stretched to apply to English. The form of an English sentence—its word order and the spelling of its verb, in particular—varies only slightly according to whether it expresses a

- fact,
- directive or command, or
- hypothesis,

which are the three strategies of sentence—different structures used to express different kinds of thought to achieve different kinds of purpose—differentiated by use of the borrowed term *mood*. The three moods, borrowed from the ancients, and distinguished in the kind of traditional grammar I learned, are these.

- Indicative: where the sentence declares a fact: He was an old man and he fished alone.
- Imperative: where the sentence issues a command, makes a direction or invitation, or even offers an emphatic kind of wish: Stop right there; Go home; Click here; Drop by on your way through; Keep me

briefed; Please tell me what to do; Get well soon; Sleep tight.

- Subjunctive: where the sentence asks a reader to imagine an ideal or hypothetical—and sometimes impossible—scenario: If I were you …; He looks at her as though she were an angel; Should he have any further questions …; We recommend that the department reform its financial systems. Note that the subjunctive mood normally occurs in a part of the sentence you will come to know as subordinate; there are only a few cases—like Bless you and God save the King, which may just as easily be seen as imperatives of the wishing kind—where the main clause of a sentence proceeds subjunctively.

It has become common to abandon the idea of mood and replace it with this distinction, which points more clearly to the purpose of the sentence:

- declarative
- interrogative
- directive
- exclamative.

This mode of analysis may be more useful because it avoids some problems of definition in the old language of mood, and because it points to the function of a sentence as a writer is likely to conceive of it. In this model, you make a sentence for one of four purposes: to declare some statement of fact; to ask a question; to demand, insist or emphatically suggest; or to exclaim. These are the four speech acts, including the acts we perform in sentences on paper.

> It's time to come down now. (Declarative)
>
> Do you think it's time to come down now? (Closed interrogative)
>
> When do you think you'll be ready to come down? (Open interrogative)
>
> Come down now. (Directive)
>
> Let's go! (Directive and exclamative)

Look at you up there alone with all those rats! (Exclamative)

To explain a couple of things: closed questions can be answered only *yes* or *no*; open questions, on the other hand, don't want a *yes* or *no*. *Where on earth is Burradoo?* can't sensibly be answered *yes*; it can be answered many ways, including *just outside Bowral. What do you want to do with your life?* is clearly an open question. On the other hand, *Is this how you imagined your life would be?* is a closed question, soliciting, in the first instance, an answer in either the affirmative or the negative. The answer may well be followed by explanation, exposition or elaboration, but that would not be the answer to the question.

The declarative mode covers the same sentences as the indicative mood, and it's a wide field. Declarative sentences state; they are the stock-in-trade of every writer. Good writing is made mostly of these. They're good for exposition, storytelling, description and most of an argument.

The rather disparate kinds of sentence once embraced under imperative mood are now spread between directives, on the one hand, and exclamations on the other. I have some more to say about the imperative mood and directive sentences in Part Two. Some exclamatives, such as *Come down now*, are shaped (verb first) like old-fashioned imperatives; others may take the form of declarations but come out as exclamations. Such an exclamation might be understood as an emphatic sort of statement, declaimed, rather than simply stated. So, the candidate, after coming back in the race for the candidacy, stands and says:

We're going on; we're going strong; we're going all the way!

Exclamations come in a variety of shapes, though; some of them aren't even proper sentences:

Damn it!

Oh, hell!

Cool!

What fools they are!

How strange this is!

Look at that!

The subjunctive disappears in this regime. Subjunctive sentences (such as *I recommend that he* get *himself a new hat*) would be considered a species of declarative sentence, in which the subordinate clause employs a verb in a particular form to express a hypothesis or wish or fancy. I have more to say about the subjunctive in Part Two.

When one starts analysing sentences for their structure, as we've begun to do here and will do in more detail below, the declarative sentence serves as the default. It is the model for naming the functional parts—the subject, predicate, object and modifier; the main and subordinate clauses; the different kinds of phrase—of any given sentence.

5

The sum of the parts

I've gone as far as I can into the natural history of sentences, without naming and defining each kind of word you'll find there. This is the grammar I learned in school, and it was about the extent of it. It's as far as most of us ever went. And it's a fair way. But knowing the names of all the pieces you're likely to find in a sentence doesn't guarantee you'll know if you have the pieces in the right order to say just the thing you meant; it's not enough to ground a sturdy understanding of how sentences function, and why you have (if you have; or haven't if you haven't) a sound sentence in front of you, and how and why the pieces change their forms, and how you put the pieces together to make the larger forms of phrase and clause, and how you order those to best effect. Knowing your parts of speech stops a step or two short of schooling a writer in the art of finding and making good the structure of a sentence. But it's a lot better than nothing. It's micro-grammar. It supplies the names for the pieces of which the larger linguistic forms—the phrase and clause—are made, and so it allows us to talk about those in detail.

To talk any more about that—to help you distinguish phrases from clauses and independent clauses from dependent clauses, which is what I need to do next—I'll have to mention nouns and verbs and pronouns, adjectives and adverbs. So here they are, and here's a summary of what they do. And while I'm about it, here are the joining words and the articles as well.

1 *Nouns* are the naming words. They take *their* name, indeed, from the Latin word for name: *nomen*. And naming is what they do. You can see how they might get used as the subject of a sentence—the thing a sentence *names*. But you'll also find them, because they name all kinds of things, acting as objects, and filling various thing-type roles in phrases and clauses. Here are some nouns on my desk or on my mind this morning:

> Glasses mug book lamp pen phone wallet peach paper dust
> mosquito scent wind grammar child love family poetry
> weather leadership solace structure poverty plenty place
> ecology Sydney Cambridge Coogee hunger mortality.

Some of these refer to objects I can see or touch, hear or smell or taste. Which ones? Nouns that point to things one can engage with through the senses are often called *concrete* nouns; such items have body; they exist in the actual world. The others—ideas, concepts, generalities—can't be understood through one's senses; to picture them one needs one's mind, with its imagination and its gift for abstract thought. So the nouns that name those things are called *abstract*. *Weather* is more abstract (because more general) than *wind*. *Love* is clearly abstract—to say nothing of *grammar*. But the line between is itself abstract and sometimes hard to see. The nouns with capital letters are called *proper* nouns; the one's without, *common*. Most of my nouns in this list were singular; some (*family*, perhaps) are *group* nouns.

But that's enough for now. There's a fair bit more to say about nouns, and I do that in Part Two.

2 *Verbs* we've introduced already. At school they were the *doing* words. They are also the *being* words. These verbs are going on where I am this morning:

> write hope sit type see hear think eat drink forget blow
> sing shake rumble imagine pass frustrate fly catch preen
> graze rest fall stand erode list analyse explain fail succeed
> distract engage ingest scent send worry stop.

Verbs come concrete and abstract, as you can see from my list: some point to activities you can or might see, touch, hear, smell or taste (*write*, *type*, *eat*, *drink*, *rumble*, *preen*, *erode*, *scent*, *send*); some, like *analyse* and *forget*, describe cerebral, invisible action, the action of the mind; *fail* is a generalising, judging verb that points, in itself, to no particular action; *sit* and *stop* describe a kind of non-action. Each of the verbs in my list is a single word; but verbs also come as verb phrases. Verbs come regular and irregular; they come transitive and intransitive. And verbs have mood and voice and tense and number. But there's too much to say about all that; I'll leave most of that for Part Two.

3 *Pronouns* stand in for nouns—hence *pro* (from the Latin for 'in place of'; *pro* meant and means other things as well—like 'in front of' and 'forward' and 'forth' and 'in favour of', but that's not what it means here!) and *noun*. You use pronouns in place of nouns. But they also stand in for phrases performing the roles that nouns perform (as subjects and objects of sentences, for the most part); they refer

sometimes to an entire clause, which may be the entire sentence before:

> He spends words all day long. *That* is why he sometimes has nothing left to say at night. (Where *that* refers to the entire first sentence.)

So I write *I* instead of the proper noun *Mark*. Instead of book, one can write, after naming it first, *it*. *She* can stand in for *my publisher*; *this* can stand in for *getting tired and grumpy* in *This is what happens when you don't go to bed early enough*. *Which* and *that* (and sometimes *who* and *what*) perform the specialised work of relative pronouns (as in ... *the book that changed my mind about everything*). There are eight families of pronouns, and some of them change their form (their spelling) according to whether they substitute for the subject or the object: *I* becomes *me* in the sentence *She commissioned me to write the report*, for instance.

These morphologies and families I deal with—notice that word order, by the way—in Part Two.

Together, nouns and verbs and pronouns are sometimes classed as the *primary parts of speech*. You need them, and you could do without anything else, to compose a sentence. They give you the plot: the thing and whatever it thinks or does or is, or whatever befalls it. They give you the *who* and the *does* and the *what* and the *to whom*.

It follows that the words that support the primary parts are sometimes called the secondaries. These words modify the primaries: *modifiers* is another name for this class of (two kinds of) word. They distinguish or describe, characterise or define the noun or the verb. They are adjectives and adverbs.

4 *Adjectives* modify nouns. Here are some adjectives—along with the nouns they affect—in my writing shed today:

> writing book, black wallet, desk lamp, old fork, snow shovel, wood stove, white chair, open window, empty cup, blue wall, concrete floor, classical music, sharp pencils, yard boots, antique watch, denim jeans, tired mind, favourite books, bird books.

Adjectives mostly fall in front of the noun they modify; when that happens they're called *prenominal* or *attributive*. Sometimes they come after it; when they do, they're called *post-nominal*, as in *The cover of the book is* yellow or *She noticed that the plant was* dead or, again, *I describe this kind of writing as* functional. When the adjective follows the verb to be (as it does in *book is yellow*), the adjective is called *predicative* because it forms part of the predicate.

Numbers in different forms also moonlight as adjectives:

> *Four Huts* (the title of a book), three blind mice, seven virtues, 800 species—*cardinal adjectives*
>
> fifth day, hundredth time, sixth degree—*ordinal adjectives*
>
> all people, most women, few children—*indefinite adjectives*

Words like *this* and *these* and *many*, which on their own are *pronouns*, become adjectives when they accompany a noun:

> *This* is the point. *This* is a pronoun, here (alluding to something just explained).
>
> He made *this* point over and over. *This* is now an adjective.
>
> *These* (pronoun) are my best boots. *These* (adjective) boots are made for walking.
>
> *Many* (pronoun) came to see the event. *Many* (adjective) people came to see the event.

Personal pronouns in their possessive forms (*my*, *your*, *her*, *his*, *our*, *your* (pl), *their*) are considered adjectives:

my turn, your book, her idea, his child, our best effort,
your failure (pl), their triumph.

Sometimes a *verb* (as a past or present participle) functions in the sentence as an adjective. *Writing* in *writing book* is an example in my list. So, too, *wrought iron*. Such verbs are called *adjectival verbs* or *gerundives*.

Nouns sometimes serve as adjectives too: *desk* lamp, *mountain* dog, *sky*scraper, *ink* well, *winter* morning, *business* report. You might also call those phrases compound nouns.

You can also compound various kinds of word to form a compound adjective: 46-year-old man (cardinal adjective + noun + adjective), middle-aged woman (noun + verb), well-tempered clavier (adverb + verb), grandly titled journal (adverb + verb). Note that these are mostly not hyphenated.

Sometimes a writer stacks a number of adjectives in front of a noun, like this: The Little Green Grammar Book, for instance, which, I suppose, contains (after the article), two adjectives (little and green) and a noun (grammar) serving as an adjective; or perhaps it amounts to two adjectives and one compound noun.

One more thing to say about the multi-dimensional adjective: most can express degrees of whatever quality they impute to the noun:

- by changing their form (*good*, *better*, *best*; *some*, *many*, *most*)
- by changing their ending (*few*, *fewer*, *fewest*; *less*, *lesser*, *least*; *green*, *greener*, *greenest*; *sad*, *sadder*, *saddest*)
- by using a helper word (*relevant*, *more relevant*, *most relevant*; *beautiful*, *more beautiful*, *most beautiful*).

Certain adjectives—*dead*, *unique*, *pregnant*, *perfect*, *unprecedented*, and *last*, for instance—cannot, by the nature or the absolute quality they express, be expressed in degrees. But that doesn't stop some of us trying.

Adjectives come in many shapes and kinds. Strictly, they are adjectival phrases unless they are made of a single word. I'll say some more about these under 'Phrases and Clauses' below.

5 *Adverbs*, the other species of modifying word, tell a reader something more about a *verb*. They refine the time, the place and the manner of the action in question. These adverbs (along with the verb they sophisticate) are going quietly about their work around me today:

> wakes early, blows northerly, writes slowly, eats fast, passes loudly, sits still, listens well, balances precariously, changes imperceptibly, works today, walks sporadically, thinks indoors, looks outside, forgets soon, remembers often, comes here, flies there, continues forever.

Adverbs that modify verbs, as you'd expect of an *adverb*, are called *adjuncts*. But not all adverbs modify verbs. Some modify adjectives; they're called *subjuncts*:

> I'm growing *slightly* weary.
>
> Grammar is *astonishingly* simple.
>
> Pavarotti's was an *utterly* glorious voice.
>
> It is *very* easy to forget that democracy depends on your vote.
>
> Adverbs are *hellishly* difficult to pin down.

Some adverbs modify other adverbs (these, too, are *subjuncts*):

> fairly well, very soon, inevitably late

Like adjectives, many adverbs express different degrees—*fast*, *faster*, *fastest*; *soon*, *sooner*, *soonest*; *lavishly*, *more lavishly*, *most lavishly*.

Adverbs may also modify an entire main clause or sentence; these adverbs are called *disjuncts*:

> Sadly, the news arrived too late to affect the decision.
>
> Happily, we have the answer to your problem.
>
> Perhaps the best idea is to start all over again.

And then there are adverbs that join two main clauses (which may or may not be sentences) together, while also distinguishing them; these are called *conjuncts* or *conjunctive adverbs*. Examples include *however*, *consequently*, *subsequently*, *significantly*, *therefore* and *thus*. I include a fuller list in the section on conjunctions below.

Conjunct adverbs often appear at the start of the second clause:

> Copperheads are well adapted to the cold; *consequently*, they don't generally hibernate in the winter, like other snakes.

They may appear—and in the case of *however* ought best to appear—after the subject of the second clause, or even later:

> This is still the bush; it's not, however, as wild as it once was.
>
> This is still the country here; it's not so much like the country as it used to be, however.

Notice the comma after, and in the last case ahead of, those conjuncts. This convention helps things make sense.

Adverbs may appear in many places in a sentence. They are not so closely bound to the word they modify as adjectives are to the nouns they normally precede.

> Today my daughter graduates.
>
> My daughter today graduates from law school.
>
> My daughter graduates today.
>
> Soon my son will wake and I will leave my desk and return

to the house.

My son will soon wake and I will leave my desk and return to the house.

My son will wake soon …

As with adjectives, much of modifying work is done not by individual adverbs but by adverbial phrases. More on this under 'The families of phrase' later in this part.

6 *Conjunctions* are joining words. *And*, *but*, *or*, *nor* and *yet* will be the ones that come to mind. But these are the *coordinating* conjunctions. They join together two words or two phrases in a clause, and they join together entire clauses—and they join them equally. Here are some coordinating conjunctions in action:

men and women

salt and pepper

hot or cold

poor but refined

Before the end but after the beginning …

I came to the plateau in the spring of 1998, and I left in the autumn of 2005.

I wanted to buy a copy of your book. But when I went to find it, the bookshop told me they'd sold out.

Note that because a conjunction is able to join two clauses, it can begin a sentence, since a sentence is, by definition, a clause. Where, as in the second last example, you compound two main clauses within one sentence, it is conventional to use a comma in front of the coordinating conjunction. The pause helps a reader hold the two ideas apart, and it avoids the suggestion that the conjunction merely joins the two words either side of it.

Subordinating conjunctions generally join two clauses, by subordinating one to the other. They make the clause they introduce subordinate to the other. These are the common subordinating conjunctions:

> because, how, however, when, where, why, whether, although, though, since, as before, after, once, till, until, whereas, if, than, for, notwithstanding.

A number of phrases also link two clauses together in the manner of subordinating conjunctions:

> as though, as if, as soon as, as far as, so that, in order to, as a consequence, by contrast, to this end, as a result, in the meantime, until now, under the circumstances.

Here are some subordinating conjunctions used in sentences:

> You need to show cause *why* I shouldn't fire you.
>
> I had always treated you *as though* you were my elder.
>
> *Because* we think so highly of your book, we are delighted to offer you a contract to publish it, *notwithstanding* our reservations about the market.

I'll supply more examples of subordinating conjunctions in sentences when I talk about *subordinate clauses* below.

7 *Prepositions* are words like *in*, *on*, *out*, *between*, *under*, *before*, *during*, *after*, *against*, *towards*, *across*, *along*, *around*, *about*, *beside*, *upon*, *into*, *near*, *off*, *of*, *by*, *down*, *up*, *through*, *from*, *within*, *without*, *at*, *like*. They appear before (pre + position) items in a sentence, and they position that item in relation to another item in the sentence.

> The cat sat *on* the mat.
>
> The car sped *towards* the exit.
>
> I promise to stand *beside* you until the end.

The air *within* the room was poised just above freezing.

She leaned *against* him; he voted *against* the bill.

The plums on the table were *for* you.

This is a poem *by* William Carlos Williams.

Prepositions describe the relationship between two items (word or phrase or even clause) in *time* (*before*, *during*, *after*) or *space* (*against*, *on*, *under*, *towards*, *between*).

Prepositions are understood as beginning a *prepositional phrase* (*towards the exit*, *beside you*, *within the room*, *against him*, *against the bill*, *for you*, *by William Carlos Williams*). Within the phrase, the noun following the preposition is said to be its object (as though the preposition were a verb); picture the noun following the preposition as *receiving* its directional or spatial force. The prepositional phrase (sometimes it might be a clause) will play the role of *modifier* (of subject, object, verb or main clause) in the sentence.

Many prepositions take the form of a phrase themselves:

pursuant to, because of, out of, next to, due to.

Some verbs require a certain preposition after them, at least in the creation of specific meanings:

appeal against, protest against [a decision; but *protest your innocence*], howl down, cater for, provide with, write to [your father; but *write your book or write down what you hear*].

Although many people still insist that *compare* must take *to* and contrast *with*, most books of contemporary usage have long allowed both usages. Likewise, *differ* may take *to* or *from*, though the American *different than* is, according to the *Macquarie Dictionary* 'widely deplored'. Nine times out of ten, one should prefer the briefer 'these things differ', anyway.

I wrote in an email to an American colleague recently that I had 'taken out' an award, and he claimed not to have heard the expression. One *takes out* the rubbish (as in 'removes'); one *takes out* a boyfriend or girlfriend (as in 'dates'); it's odd, I guess, that in the Australian vernacular one can also *take out* a prize (as in 'win' it).

Take out is an example, in any event, of a *phrasal verb*: a verb + preposition compound where the preposition inflects the verb with a particular meaning. Pam Peters contrasts *He ran up a big hill* (where *up* is a preposition introducing a phrase that modifies, adverbially, the verb) with *He ran up a big bill* (where, effectively, the verb is *ran up*, the preposition being inseparable from the verb).

8 This leaves us (excluding the hybrids I've already mentioned) with *articles*: *the* and *a* (which is sometimes *an*). Contemporary grammar regards articles as a subset of a larger class of words called *determiners*. Other determiners are *each*, *all*, *several*, *many*, *seven*, *no* and *any*; most of them are pronouns in their other life. Let's stick to *the*, *a* and *an* for now. I'll run through determiners at the tail of my fuller treatment of pronouns in the next part of the book.

Many language systems, of which English, German and French are examples, use articles to *signal* nouns.

You don't use an article every time you use a noun. When you don't, the noun in question, standing all on its own, operates at a general level. Compare *The women wanted to vote* with *Women wanted to vote*. *Dogs are four-legged mammals* talks about the class of animal called *dog*. *The dogs are barking* means dogs of the writer's acquaintance are barking. *Dogs are barking* means some dogs, unknown to the writer, or whose particular identity and ownership need not concern us, are barking.

Article is hard to define, except to say it's a word that works as a kind of modifier—not a very specific one, but a modifier, all the same—that singles out one *boy* or *woman*, *hospital* or *car* from the general class of *boys*, *women*, *hospitals* and *cars*.

The is more specific than *a*. So, *the* is referred to as *the definite article*. *A* is *the indefinite article*.

> *The boy* narrows the field more than *a boy*. Similarly, *the car* is more definite than *a car*; *the hospital* is more definite than *a hospital*.

The will be read as referring to a noun already identified or about to be identified or understood as being somehow more particular. In other words, if I write 'the boy', you will read it as a reference to a boy who has some connection with me, at least in this sentence. *A*, by contrast, signifies a noun, let's say a *child*, connected, in this sentence, to no one—floating and anonymous.

> A boy drove the car to the hospital.
>
> The boy drove a car to a hospital.
>
> The boy drove the car to hospital.

Hospital, without either *a* or *the*, as in the last example, doesn't want you to think of a particular hospital—either with or without any connection to the boy. It is almost adverbial, as in *for help*.

The indefinite article *a* is pronounced either *ae* or something more like *uhh*, as in *a hundred years ago*. In either case, it's hard to jump, in speech, from that vowel sound to another vowel sound, at the start of the following noun—as in *a apple*. For this reason, when the noun begins with a *vowel* (*a*, *e*, *i*, *o*, *u*) one adds an *n* to the indefinite article, making it *an*:

> an architect
>
> an egg
>
> an idea
>
> an organ
>
> an umbrella.

When the *u* sounds like *you*, as it does in *uniform*, it effectively (phonetically) starts with the consonant *y*—so you would drop the *n*:

a uniform, a universal choice, a ukulele.

The general rule, then, is: use *an* before nouns that start with a *vowel*; use *a* before nouns that start with a consonant. But the rule, as you see, has to do with the sound of the thing, so be subtle.

The *h* in *historian* and *hotel*, for instance, sounds like a consonant, and should be preceded by *a*, whereas the *h* in *honour* and *hour* is pretty much silent, so that the word sounds as though it begins with a vowel. So, it's *an honour* and *an hour*.

Beware acronyms or abbreviations. *NZ* starts with a consonant, but it sounds like *enzed*; so you'd write *an NZ*. By contrast, *US* starts with a vowel that sounds like a consonant—*you-ess*; so you'd write *a US*.

6

Communities of words—phrases and clauses

Most sentences aren't made of words alone; the units that compose them are often word groups. Most sentences don't proceed as sparely as these, and we wouldn't get far if they did:

He writes speeches.

Clouds drop rain.

The girls wore summer dresses and walked the beach slowly.

We recommend immediate action.

Each of these is made of words, not word groups—unless one wants to call *the girls* and *the beach* phrases. Each sentence is grammatically simple, being made of only one main clause. That clause is, of course, itself a word group—but each of its pieces stands on its own; each word there is, all by itself, a subject, verb, object or modifier. But it's hard to say much that's very subtle without the help of some helper words and some phrases; you can't get far without making some word groups to serve in one or more of the four roles on offer. Any group of words bunched together (more than one word will do it), each of which belongs more to that group than to another word in the sentence—this is what I mean by a word cluster. Like individual words, word clusters may perform one of the roles on offer in a sentence: subject, verb, object or modifier. And a word cluster is either a *phrase* or a *clause*. Let me add some word clusters (both phrases and clauses) to those sentences to show you what happens and how they work and what they add.

> He writes speeches for the CEO. *For the CEO* is a modifying phrase.
>
> When the meteorological conditions are right, clouds drop rain from their bases. *When the meteorological conditions are right* is a modifying clause; *from their bases* is a modifying phrase.
>
> The girls in their summer dresses walked the beach like shorebirds. *In their summer dresses* becomes a modifying phrase (it modifies the subject); *like shorebirds* is a modifying phrase (a simile).
>
> Because of what our audit unearthed, we recommend immediate action by the department to secure managerial independence. *Because of what our audit unearthed* is a modifying phrase (serving as an introduction); *by the department* and *to secure managerial independence* are both modifiers, the first a prepositional phrase, the second an infinitive phrase.

PHRASES AND CLAUSES

A phrase is a word group without a subject or a predicate or both.

To change me is a phrase on both counts, lacking a subject and having only a verb in the infinitive; since the verb is not finite, the word group has no predicate. It's a phrase—an infinitive phrase, to be exact.

Ducking and weaving would also be a phrase (not a clause) because it has neither a finite verb nor a subject. *After midnight* sounds like a modifier; it contains a preposition and its object (the noun *midnight*); but without a subject or a verb of any kind, it's just a phrase.

By contrast, *a clause is word group containing both a subject and a predicate.* That, you may recall, is also the definition I offered for the sentence at the start. It follows, that unless a clause is made *dependent* (*subordinate* is the other word for this) by one means or another—by a subordinating conjunction or by a relative pronoun (*which*, *that*, *who*)—it will be an *independent clause* and therefore also a sentence.

> *She changed me* becomes an independent clause because now it has a subject (*She*) and a finite verb (*changed*).
>
> *She wants to change me* also becomes an independent clause because it has, now, a subject (*she*) and a predicate (*wants to change me*) including a finite verb (*wants*), and an infinitive clause (*to change me*), serving, within the predicate, either as the object of the verb (*wants*), or as its complement (*wants to change me* being regarded as a special case by most modern grammarians; it's called the *catenative construction*—see Huddleston 2005, p 214)
>
> *He was ducking and weaving* also becomes an independent clause when it gets a subject (*he*) and when its verbs are made finite (*was ducking*).

A phrase, like a word alone, is a subset of a clause. Clauses, as defined here, are made of units; some of the units are words; some of the units are those lesser word clusters known as phrases. Sometimes, a phrase stands outside and modifies a clause, all on its own:

> *In the beginning* God created the heavens and the earth.

In the beginning is the phrase here, and *God created the heavens and the earth* is the independent clause. But because the modifier is not a clause, not even a dependent clause, it is understood as belonging inside the clause.

There are many kinds of phrase—*in the beginning* is a prepositional phrase—and phrases may fill any of the four roles on offer in a sentence—as subject, verb, object or modifier.

What counts with a clause—in terms of its self-sufficiency and how you punctuate it—is whether it's independent. Knowing your independent from your dependent clause will tell you where to put the commas; and it will tell you where the central story is told. And that is a matter of importance both rhetorically and aesthetically—that is, you want, in most functional writing anyway, to make your main point in your main clause, to give it the right emphasis; but you also want, for reasons of style, to make many different kinds of sentence structure. The difference between them often turns on how many, and which, clauses you make independent, and how you join them with other clauses—through subordination of some, or through coordination.

7

The families of phrase

There are five kinds of phrase:

- prepositional phrase—a word cluster that starts with a preposition: *in this report*, *with a preposition*, *after much thought*, *under the circumstances*
- verbal phrase—a word cluster with a verb as head word (combining to form a verb): *will finish*, *work up*, *to decide for oneself*
- noun phrase—a word cluster with a noun as head word (combining to form a noun): *word cluster*, *the new government*, *The Little Green Grammar Book*
- adjectival phrase—a word cluster with an adjective as head word (combining to form an adjective): *very fine*, *smoke-filled*, *ten-year-old*
- adverbial phrase—a word cluster with an adverb as head word (combining to form an adverb): *more urgently*, *less significantly*.

And phrases, as I mentioned, can perform all four functions in a sentence:

- subject—*Improving your sentences* improves yourself
- verb—The government *will be signing* the treaty
- object—I have written *the writing book*
- modifier—*In the last financial year*, we got out of the financial woods; the struggle *to improve our sentences* is the struggle *to improve ourselves*.

PREPOSITIONAL PHRASES

Prepositional phrases (a preposition plus its object) mostly work as modifiers. They modify nouns:

> Life *on the land* keeps one close to the essence of things.

Here, *on the land* explains the kind of *life* (noun) we're talking about. *Life on the land* (noun + prepositional phrase) also constitutes a *noun phrase*, which serves as the subject of the sentence.

They modify verbs:

> We live here *by design*, not *by accident*.

By design modifies *live*; *by accident* modifies (*not*) *live*.

> The rats get in *through the gap between the roof and the wall.*
>
> *At dawn* he rose and fed the chooks.

In the first, *through the gap* introduces a long prepositional phrase, which includes a second: *between... Through the gap* modifies the phrasal verb *get in*; *between the roof and the wall* modifies the noun *gap*.

At dawn modifies the verb *rose*, on a strict reading. More loosely, it seems, like many prepositional phrases that serve as introductions, to modify (as in *introduce*) the whole clause. No matter what, precisely, one thinks they modify, modifying is what they do. One might call such phrases—even single-word modifiers, like *happily* and *inevitably*—*supplements* (see Huddleston, p 79).

Occasionally, you'll find a prepositional phrase serving as the *subject*:

> *Under the eaves* is where the birds roost.

Or as the subject complement:

> Where the birds roost is *under the eaves*.

VERBAL PHRASES

At its simplest, a verbal phrase is a cluster of words together forming a verb—a kind of compound verb, made up of two or more verbs or of a verb and another part of speech or two. There are a few species.

Phrasal verbs are verbs that employ a verb and a following *particle* (usually a preposition, or even two) to express the action they're trying to describe:

> break through, break down, break up, break in, act up, act out, speak up, speak up about, speak out, speak down to, play out, play up, get up, get out, get over, work up, work out, work over, make up, make over, make out, take out, pick up, put down, turn on, turn off, turn up, turn down, turn in, turn out, look up, look out on, look out for, look into, look over, look down on, wash up, give up, give out, give in, give over, face up to, give in to, walk out on, meet up with.

Both (or all three) words combine to express the action in question; together they constitute the phrasal verb, this first species of verbal phrase. Phrasal verbs sound like speech; they are quite proper, but informal. So they belong in the kind of style I believe in, the intelligent vernacular. Sometimes you could find a shorter way through another verb. *I phoned her up* can be *I phoned her*. *We have come up with* could become *we have developed*, which uses fewer words, though no fewer syllables. *Let's get out of here* could be *Let's go*.

Verbals, just to distinguish them, are verb forms lacking an auxiliary verb to make them grammatically complete; if they were complete, they would be instances of the second meaning of the term *verb phrase*—compound verbs made up of two or more verbs. The verb forms in question will be the past participle (*damaged*) or the present participle (*damaging*) of the verb.

Here are some verbals, used in their two functions, as nouns (known as *gerunds* in the present participle) and modifiers (*gerundives*):

> *Dancing* is addictive—*dancing* is a noun here, the subject of the sentence.
>
> I went to the pool to watch the *swimming*—*swimming* is a noun here, the object of the sentence.
>
> An *improved* performance—*improved* is a past participle serving as an adjective.
>
> In *breaking* news—*breaking* is a gerundive serving as an adjective.

If we take those verbals and add auxiliary verbs (more on them under 'Verbs') and use them in a sentence, we'd make these verb phrases:

> The girl was dancing.
>
> Come August, the team will be swimming at the Olympics.
>
> Her performance had been improved by new training techniques.
>
> The jets are breaking the sound barrier.

The verb in its infinite form (the verb in its dictionary form + *to*, indicating complete tenselessness) is also a verb phrase: *to change*, *to make*, *to walk*, *to buy*, *to watch*, *to sing*, *to manufacture* and so on. You'd call these *infinitive phrases*. You'd call them *infinitive phrases* when they have an object, too: *to change her*, *to make trouble*, *to walk home*, *to buy groceries*, *to sing hymns*, *to manufacture meaning*.

Infinitive phrases work as nouns and modifiers (adjectives and adverbs):

To err is human; *to forgive*, divine (Alexander Pope)—each infinitive is a noun (and the subject of its clause).

What she wanted more than anything was *to write*—where the infinite verbal phrase is a subject complement.

The effort *to win*—*to win* modifies the noun *the effort* in this noun phrase.

To finish, let me just say—*to finish* might be understood as modifying the whole clause or the verb within it.

The right *to decide* for oneself—*to decide* modifies the noun *right*.

Infinites (as one sees in this list) marry some adjectives and nouns to form phrases like these:

happy to hear, wonderful to know, hard to like, easy to forget, certain to fail, decision to separate, order to leave, recommendation to change, time to remember, someone to tell.

And infinitive phrases convey purpose; it's a leaner way of writing *in order to*:

I've come to this place *to belong*.

We walked to the river *to fish*.

He stood up *to speak*.

He went out *to change the world*.

The grammar of certain complicated (but very common) verbal phrases—especially those combining finite verbs and nonfinite verbs, as in *For years she laboured* ***to perfect*** *her voice* and *He asked us* ***to attempt to answer*** *the question*—is still being settled, believe it or not.

The books call the *laboured to perfect/ wanted to leave/ seemed to want/ tried to avoid* construction *catenative*; the common interpretation is that the infinitive verb is the *complement* of the finite verb in front of it (called, because of its support role, *auxiliary*); any noun that follows would, I think, be seen as the object of the complete verbal phrase. But what about *He asked us to attempt* or *She wanted us to leave*, where a pronoun object intervenes between the first part of the verbal phrase and the second? Even Pam Peters isn't sure (p 119); Huddleston treats them as *complex catenatives*. That'll do, I suppose. But it feels to me as though the infinitive phrase then complements or even modifies the object of the first verb, rather than the auxiliary verb.

Here are some of these more complicated forms:

> Philippa *seemed to convince* the committee.
>
> Philippa *wanted to convince* the committee.
>
> She *convinced* the committee *to publish* the book.
>
> I *watched* her *being led* to the gallows.
>
> We *need to get* the treaty *signed*.

Pam Peters notes (p 788) that, in mainstream contemporary grammatical thought, the entire *predicate* of a clause may be referred to as a *verb phrase*, which is not, perhaps, the same thing as a *verbal phrase*. Huddleston's book is an example of this approach. He gives this example,

> Cats like water,

describing *like* + *water* as the VP, that is, the verb phrase, and predicate; he then calls *like* the 'verb' and 'predicator', and *water* the 'object' and 'noun phrase'.

I'm not sure it helps to call the *predicate* anything else than the *predicate*, so I won't be calling it a 'verb phrase' here. (I should also note that the usage *noun phrase* for a noun, when it is a single word, doesn't make much sense to me. I don't employ it here, even though Pam Peters and many others do these days.)

The last kind of *verbal phrase* to mention is the *nonfinite verbal phrase*. Such a phrase starts with a verb, or has a verb as its head word; often that verb is a *verbal* (a past or present participle). Each such phrase is shorthand for a subordinate clause, but one lacking the usual device (such as *who were* or *which was* or *by*) by which a clause is made a subordinate.

Here's an example:

> The findings, *established by thorough investigation and the application of impeccable logic*, established the need for reform in the sector.

The italicised verbal phrase lacks a subject (*which*) and an auxiliary verb (*were*) to make it strictly a clause. But most grammarians read it, and phrases like it, as a shorthand form of the full verbal clause; they treat such nonfinite verbal phrases, therefore, as *verbal clauses*. In my example, the verbal word cluster, whether we call it a clause or a phrase, functions as a modifier. Here are some more *nonfinite verbal phrases/clauses*. Notice that they nearly always lack a subject, which they borrow (*they* in the first; *he* in the second) from the main clause.

> *Having left the city behind*, they soon forgot everything that had seemed so essential about it.
>
> *Working ten hours a day for two weeks*, he got the report written by the deadline.
>
> For many employees *entering the workforce*, the biggest challenge is learning how to write.
>
> *Born angry*, she spent her adult years practising calm.

When they had left is how the first translates into the language of the clause; *because he worked*, in the second; *who enter the workforce* or *when they enter the workforce*, in the third; born angry is really *having been born angry* or *because she was born angry*.

NOUN PHRASES

Noun phrase means a cluster of words with a noun as its head word. It may be something as small as *the book* or *a report* or something as long (and awkward) as:

> *The existing and future needs of local citizens for access to local open space* are considered by *specially appointed representatives of the council's subcommittee for the management of new developments on public properties.*

Within the noun phrase may be other phrases, such as the prepositional phrases *to local open space* and *of new developments*, as well as adjectival phrases such as *specially appointed*.

Noun phrases, because they are really just elongated nouns, can perform the functions performed by nouns (and pronouns): the *subject* and the *object*, the *subject complement*, *object complement* and *appositive*.

> Daniel Slager, the CEO of Milkwood Editions, today signed the essayist, Annie Prose.

The subject is the noun phrase *Daniel Slager*; *the CEO of Milkwood Editions* is a noun phrase (including a prepositional phrase), serving as an appositive of the subject; *the essayist* is a noun phrase working as the *object*; *Annie Prose* is the appositive (noun phrase) of the *object*.

An *appositive* is a phrase that sits beside a subject or object, or other noun in the sentence, and offers more information (often a name or a title or job description) about it. It is not an additional subject or object or noun; it puts the same thing another way. Functionally, in a sense, appositives modify; but in their form and structure, they remain noun phrases, so it is as though they are, themselves the subject or object (or other noun—expressed in other words).

> Daniel Slager is the CEO of the press.
>
> Annie Prose is the world's best essayist.

Here *the CEO of the press* is the subject complement of the noun phrase *Daniel Slager*; *the world's best essayist* complements the subject *Annie Prose*.

ADJECTIVAL AND ADVERBIAL PHRASES

These are simply compound adjectives or adverbs. That is, they are small clusters of words, the headword of which is, in the one case, an adjective, in the other, an adverb, but in any event, a modifying word. Some of them will be expressions that might be translated with a single modifying word:

> in every way, at random, on rotation, without reservation, on a regular basis, to a certain extent, up to a point, after due consideration, in a manner of speaking.

Others are the compounds one makes to express the degree of the adjective or adverb:

> more frightened, most eligible, very judiciously.

Others are the kinds of compounds I noted when I was talking about adjectives earlier. These may combine many parts of speech, but their headword or their function in the sentence will be modifying (adjectival or adverbial):

> absolutely unbelievable, partially completed, world's best practice, quality assured, well drained, smoke infused, black letter, four letter, seventh generation, only partially, frankly disrespectful, unusually absent-mindedly.

8

The five canonical clauses

A clause, again, is a subject and a predicate, and within the predicate you'll find a finite verb. Clauses come dependent and independent. But before we talk about the varieties of dependent clause and the kinds of sentence one can make using a mix of dependent and independent clauses, you should know that there are five 'canonical' structures of independent clause. (I note that the canon excludes directive, exclamatory and interrogative sentence structures; but we've looked at those already.) These five structures are what you can make with just one clause of a declarative sentence. Everyone agrees that there are these five structures; I follow Huddleston's nomenclature and analysis.

A ORDINARY INTRANSITIVE (SUBJECT + INTRANSITIVE VERB)

The storm broke.

He will laugh; she will cry.

The hens panicked.

The rain eases.

The world will end.

The verb makes up the entire predicate. It's called *intransitive* because it communicates its meaning to no one or nothing. It just happens. Full stop.

B COMPLEX INTRANSITIVE (SUBJECT + VERB + SUBJECT COMPLEMENT/MODIFIER)

The officer felt angry.

It seemed ridiculous.

The child will lie perfectly still.

The weather was mild.

The end result is violence.

In some of these, the subject complement is an adjective; in others, it's a noun. In some cases, the verb is the verb *to be*, which never takes an object, serving instead to link the subject with a subject complement element of the sentence—to identify one with the other. In other cases, the verb is something else (*to feel*, *to seem*, *to lie*); but it works intransitively, and the noun or adjective modifies it.

C ORDINARY TRANSITIVE (SUBJECT + VERB + DIRECT OBJECT)

She sees me.

I finally finished the book.

Siegfried fixed the gutter.

The government will break its election promises.

The eastern spinebills built their nest.

Where, as here, the verb works transitively, it inflicts itself on an object (noun or noun phrase or pronoun).

D COMPLEX TRANSITIVE (SUBJECT + VERB + OBJECT + OBJECT COMPLEMENT)

He makes her sad.

She loved the writer A D Hope.

Everyone thought this a tragedy.

E DITRANSITIVE (SUBJECT + VERB + OBJECT + INDIRECT OBJECT)

I gave you some breakfast.

They emailed me the documents.

She wrote the government a letter.

The postman hands the parcel to me.

Tonight I'll read the children a book.

One can add modifying words and phrases to these structures, and they will keep their integrity (*They emailed the documents to me in Germany*; *On Sunday, I finally finished my first book of poems*). Each will remain an independent clause unless it is subordinated by a word or phrase like *because* or *whether* or *when* or *no matter why*. Unless it is so subordinated, it stands on its own as a sentence. When one adds a subordinate clause to any of the examples in any of these five structures, one makes a complex sentence.

> Tonight, I'll read the children a book *that I loved as a child.*
>
> *When they split up*, everyone thought it was a tragedy.

9

A brief history of dependency—dependent clauses and their uses

A dependent (or subordinate) clause is a clause that falls short of autonomy. Such clauses, like those italicised just above, function as dependent elements in larger and more sophisticated sentence structures; they flesh out and are sustained by main clauses. Unlike independent clauses, they aren't sentences on their own; they modify or somehow add to main (independent) clauses. Subordinate clauses act as *modifiers* (adjectival or adverbial) or as *noun clauses* (playing the role of subject, object or complement).

A subordinate clause contains a subject and predicate, like a main clause, but there is something about it that makes it incompetent. Generally, a subordinate clause begins with a word or phrase that subordinates it; mostly, that word is a *subordinating conjunction* or a *relative pronoun*.

But for this inequality of clauses—this dependence of some clauses on others—every sentence would be more or less the same thing; no clause would carry more weight than any other. The geography of paragraphs would be flatter and the soil poorer.

Here are some dependent clauses. Hear them calling out for main clauses?

> That Jack built
>
> Because I can't find anyone else
>
> While we're standing here talking about independent clauses
>
> However you look at this problem
>
> Whether this is what the government intended
>
> If you come by tomorrow
>
> After you've mastered the art of the sentence
>
> That he loved her, too
>
> How it came about

What subordinates each of these is the word that begins it. With one exception, if you took that word away, you'd be left with a sentence. The exception is the first. It's a relative clause, and generally, the word that starts a relative clause is part of that clause, serving as either its subject or object. *That* is the object of this one. But if you replace *that* in the first of my list of dependent clauses with the pronoun *it*—and reverse the word order so the subject *Jack* comes first—you get this sentence: *Jack built it*.

Let's join those subordinate clauses to main clauses and make some (complex) sentences:

> This is the house *that Jack built*.
>
> *Because I can't find anyone else,* I'm going to ask you to marry me.
>
> *While we're standing here talking about independent clauses*, let me give you an example of one.
>
> *However you look at this problem*, we're stuck with it.

It's hard to work out *whether this is what the government intended.*

You might find me in a better mood *if you come by tomorrow.*

After you've mastered the art of the sentence, there's not all that much left to learn.

She saw *that he loved her, too.* (This one is called a *content clause*; it serves to flesh the main clause out; the subordinate clause serves as the object of the verb.)

How it came about was a bit of an accident. (Here, the subordinate clause serves as the subject of the sentence.)

Each of these sentences joins two ideas—two clause stories—by stressing one and de-stressing the other. We do something similar, though smaller scale, when we emphasise certain syllables in a word, and then in a phrase, over others. The effect is not just rhetorical—in the sense of giving more importance to one thought, and less to the other. The effect is also musical. Sentences made of main and subordinate clauses have more topography—more rise and fall—than simple or compound sentences. A writer can put this to work in the composition—in the vernacular, semantic music—that is her writing.

Hear how differently the sentences I made above—by subordinating one part of them to the other—sound when I simply conjoin them. They don't really *mean* anything different; they just *sound* different. And difference, diversity and variation are subtle but important writing values.

This is the house, and Jack built it.

I can't find anyone else; I'm going to ask you to marry me.

We're standing here talking about independent clauses. Let me give you an example of one.

Look at this problem: we're stuck with it.

Is this is what the government intended? It's hard to work out.

Come by tomorrow, and you might find me in a better mood.

> You've mastered the art of the sentence; there's not all that much left to learn.
>
> She saw it: he loved her, too.
>
> It came about by accident.

There's nothing much wrong with any of these sentences. Some of them sound better, some more awkward, than they did when I joined their two parts using subordination. But they're not, by virtue of their structure, either better or worse than those made using subordination. The thing to notice is that there are many ways (four, in fact) to link one's clauses, and a good writer uses them all.

But before we look at those four sentence structures, let's talk some more about subordination.

SUBORDINATION ONE—SUBORDINATING CONJUNCTIONS

I mentioned *subordinating conjunctions* in my miscellany of the parts of speech; they are, of course, a species of conjunction (alongside *coordinating conjunctions*). Now we see what they're for. They are the first category of word (and phrase) that can subordinate one clause to another. I listed some of them earlier. Here are a few used in sentences.

> *Although* you had expected another poet, I hope I won't disappoint you.
>
> She turned and looked at her husband *as though* she had never seen him before.
>
> I thought Brown was the best horseman in the country *until* I saw you.
>
> *Unless* you have a better idea, I say we eat at the Thai place on Railway Street.
>
> *While* I have read more saleable books, I've never read one so beautiful.

SUBORDINATION TWO—RELATIVE PRONOUNS

There is a class of pronouns called *relative pronouns*, and they are the second kind of word capable of subordinating a clause.

On most occasions, the relative pronouns are *which*, *that* and *who*. Others are *what*, *whoever* and *whatever*. Sometimes *where* and *when* perform the role. Relative pronouns are so called because they relate the words that follow them (the rest of the subordinate clause they commence) back to one particular word or phrase that precedes them. Effectively, they delay a modifying word cluster until the word it modifies has been said, a thing one wants to do from time to time—because it is of some length and would interrupt the flow of the main clause if we put it there, or because you want to emphasise it.

> Today the party announces its education policy, *which will be the springboard to our re-election.*
>
> These are just the few things *that I haven't yet forgotten about love.*
>
> She found the house *that her mother had lived in as a child.*
>
> The chickens, *which had spent the day free-ranging the house paddock*, returned to their roost at dusk.

Mostly the relative clause modifies a word in the main clause. It ought to modify the noun or noun phrase that appears directly before it, otherwise the relative clause will dangle.

> The government has introduced an advertising campaign highlighting the dangers of certain recreational drugs which it hopes will capture the attention of the young demographic that uses them.

Here, the writer probably meant to say that the government hopes its ad campaign, not the drugs, will capture the hearts and minds of the young; she meant the subordinate clause *which it hopes will capture* ... to describe the noun phrase *advertising campaign*. Putting the modifier in the wrong place—dangling *which it hopes* after *recreational drugs*—leads a reader to the wrong conclusion. Oops. Try two sentences. Organise each sentence so the relative clause abuts the main clause, with the relative pronoun following immediately upon the noun it modifies.

Sometimes the relative clause relates to the whole clause that precedes it. Generally, these constructions are conversational, which is fine, if not especially elegant.

> I received a good offer today to publish my book, which, of course, is a huge relief.
>
> They decided to move to the country, which was a big surprise to everyone who knew them.

One would always put a comma ahead of such a relative clause, and it would start with *which* not *that*.

Because relative pronouns serve as the subject or object of the clause they begin, a couple of them (*who* and *whoever*) change their form when they are playing the object.

> I will choose whomever I like best.
>
> She is the woman whom my friend fell in love with at college.

Relative clauses come in two varieties: *restrictive* and *nonrestrictive*, depending on whether the relative clause defines or describes the relevant noun. A *restrictive relative clause* defines that noun; a nonrestrictive one merely describes it, by adding some additional, but inessential information about it. A *restrictive* (or *defining*) relative pronoun delays a clause essential to the meaning you want the word so modified to make; it aims to restrict the meaning that noun would have on its own. Here's an example:

> You are entering an area that contains steep cliffs and dangerous edges.

Without the words introduced by the relative pronoun, the sign has said nothing meaningful, nothing worth taking notice of at all: *You are entering an area*. Well, yes. The relative clause is defining.

Nonrestrictive clauses merely describe. Here's an example of one I gave you before:

The chickens, which had spent the day free-ranging the house paddock, returned to their roost at dusk.

Fowler once strongly commended *that* for use in introducing *restrictive relative clauses*, though he noted that it was far from a universal practice even among the better writers. In American letters, Fowler's preference has hardened into a firm principle. Strunk & White suggest going on a *which* hunt for all those *which*es doing *that* work. Microsoft's grammar checker insists upon the distinction. My wife, who had a Brisbane education, inflected with much more American literature and style than my Anglophone Sydney schooling, grew up using *that* to define and *which* (always with a comma) to describe. I notice, in my reading, that American writers of the finest kind—writers for *The New Yorker*, for instance—generally observe the distinction and use *that* as though it were good style; they use the odd *which* where a *that*, according to the Fowler–Strunk–Microsoft rubric, ought really to go; and they use *that* far more than British and Australian writers of similar distinction, many of whom use so few *that*s it's clear they bear it some animus. Many of us pick up a message at school that *that* does not belong in nice society. This is a message of similar merit to those other silly ideas, often fiercely insisted upon: *you can't start a sentence with 'and' or 'but'; you can't end a sentence with a preposition; you should never split your infinitives*.

For myself, while trying to avoid the kind of dogma that has let—to my ears—*which* get out of its box and given *that* a bad press, I like to observe the Fowler rule. I keep *which* for only those occasions where it clearly calls for a comma in front of it because it introduces additional information; I use *that* for all *defining* clauses. It's probably what I've trained my ears to hear, but *that*, in its trimness and soft insistence, seems to make the right kind of sound for coupling clauses—almost like carriages—so they don't come apart in anyone's mind. Equally, *which* sounds kind of slow and 'take it or leave it; this is just an afterthought' to me. That sign I quoted earlier, *which*, as it happens, I encountered on a track at Minnamurra Falls, actually read thus:

> You are entering an area which contains steep clifflines and dangerous edges.

Manifestly, it is not meant to be read as *You are entering an area, which contains...* (To write *you are entering an area. It contains ...* , which that usage implies, is dopey.) *Which* in other words introduces a *restrictive clause*. So, I wanted the sign to read:

> You are entering an area that contains steep cliffs and dangerous edges.

It is the coolness and stylish utility, the vernacular toughness of *that* I want to defend—its fitness for the specific purpose Fowler, too, thought it well made for. On my reading, the overuse of *which* in Australia and the United Kingdom is a post-Second World War phenomenon; it coincides with a tailing off of the teaching of grammar and style in those two countries.

Which is overused on the basis of a bias against *that*, a word many students are foolishly taught at school to disdain, along with *got* and *but*. There's a degree of unreconstructed bad attitude—a bit of prissiness and pomp—about the overuse of *which*. It's one more small means by which Australian writers, particularly in high-end policy and commercial documents, inflect their writing with a formality quite unnecessary, indeed unhelpful, to the meaning they are trying to make and the professional tone they are trying to strike. *Which* is a sibilant habit, I think, like *assist* and *amongst* and *whilst*. And like those words, *which* is often favoured by people who don't write much or don't write easily; in documents like kindergarten newsletters and letters to and from the local council, *which* abounds and betrays anxiety. Proper writing, you sense these writers thinking, must call for a proper-sounding word like *which*.

I need to acknowledge that sensible authorities like Pam Peters and the *Style Manual* allow either *which* or *that* for restrictive relative clauses, but I suggest you favour *that* for clauses like these—for restrictive relative clauses:

> Orange was the only area in the State *that* recorded any rainfall for the twenty-four hours to nine o'clock.
>
> This is the house *that* Jack built.
>
> These are the strategies *that* we need to pursue if we are not merely to survive and contain, but to prosper from climate change.

Keep your *which*es for clauses like these—clauses you pause in front of:

> The book, which had sat on his shelf unread for years, changed his life the moment he opened it.
>
> We will call you tomorrow on 612 9898 8181, which is the number you advised us to use.
>
> This policy statement explains ASIC's reforms to existing insider trading laws, which have come under pressure recently because of the advent of new financial instruments such as calls option.
>
> The cottage, which had housed the families of three generations of dairy farmers, now housed mine.

That has no history in such clauses. No one uses *that* to open *nonrestrictive relatives*—the native habitat of *which*. But we oughtn't to let it run wild. Something in me, like something in grumpy old Strunk, wants to make this business simpler. I think we'd think straighter about our connections—defining or descriptive; necessary or additional—if we did. If you want to define—use *that*, as we do in *the house that Jack built*. If you want to add some colour—use *which*, and put a comma in front of it.

Regardless of whether you choose *which* or *that* for restrictive clauses, it is always acceptable—and advisable—to drop the word out when it is the *object* of its clause. (In my reading, when a relative pronoun can be dropped, it was *that* in the first place; having deftly and definitively married the two clauses, it drops away.)

Thus:

> Those were the reasons [that] the judge gave for his harsh sentence.
>
> This is the place [that] they moved to when the city got too much—in every sense—for them.
>
> These are the strategies [that] we need to pursue if we are not merely to survive and contain, but to prosper from climate change.
>
> She is the woman [whom] my friend fell in love with at college.

Notice that it's still polite to use *who* (or *whom*, the form it took in that last sentence, before it was dropped) when the relative clause refers to a person.

> The teacher who spoke at last year's conference is a friend of mine. (This is a *that* kind of *who*.)

The *Style Manual* (p 74) offers the following illustration of how carefully a writer must think through and then punctuate her relative clauses. Sometimes, your whole meaning hangs on how clearly you indicate whether your subordinate clause is defining or descriptive. Whenever there may be confusion, revert to the Fowler principle—or recast your clauses to avoid the problem.

Consider the different meanings these three sentences make—each made of more or less the same words deployed in the same order. Notice how the careless use of *which* produces the ambiguity.

1 *The findings that were likely to cause embarrassment were not circulated.* (This means that some of the findings were likely to cause embarrassment, and those findings were not circulated.)

2 *The findings, which were likely to cause embarrassment, were not circulated.* (This means that none of the findings was circulated because all of them were likely to embarrass people.)

3 *The findings which were likely to cause embarrassment were not circulated.*

(Without the commas, turning the relative clause into a parenthetic, this most likely means the same as the first; but it sounds more like the second, and, especially since people are casual about their use of commas, could easily be read as meaning the same as the second.)

That unambiguously *defines*; *which* (after a comma) unambiguously *describes*; but *which*, acting as *that*, can confuse us. The point is: be careful to say what you think you mean. If in doubt, try two independent clauses:

> Some of the findings were likely to cause embarrassment; we didn't circulate those.

Or join the two clauses more clearly:

> Because the findings were likely to cause embarrassment, we didn't circulate them.

Here's another example I recently came across in some work I was editing:

> These findings have been confirmed by other post-occupancy studies which indicate that patients and families who use hospital gardens report positive mood changes and reduced stress.

Now, if *which* is meant to be restrictive in that sentence, as the absence of a comma would imply, the sentence means, if I may paraphrase,

> The findings have been confirmed by studies that establish that patients and families who use hospital gardens experience a better vibe.

The findings, by the way, are that nurses and healthcare workers get health benefits from using green space in hospitals; so, if the sentence is to be understood restrictively, it amounts to a circular argument. So I assumed it was meant to be read the other way, nonrestrictively; and I put in the comma.

> These findings have been confirmed by other post-occupancy studies, which indicate that patients and families who use hospital gardens report positive mood changes and reduced stress.

It seems to me that many writers would benefit—and so would their readers—from keeping *which* for nonrestrictive clauses. If you do this, you only ever use *which* with a comma in front of it, and no one, least of all you, gets confused. *That*, then, as ever, is only for restrictive clauses, and never wants a comma.

Confusion reigns, and I'd rather sound prescriptive than further it. Okay. I'm getting down from here now.

Other relative pronouns

Sometimes the adverbs *where* and *when* introduce relative clauses (of the *that*, or *restrictive*, kind):

> This is the place where you were born.
>
> This is the moment when you must decide to leave or to stay.

In each of these cases (and perhaps all cases) the adverb begins a restrictive relative clause and really stands in for *that*. For this reason, it can drop away when, as here, it is the object of the relative clause.

SUBORDINATION THREE—COMPARATIVE AND CONTENT CLAUSES

Huddleston and other contemporary grammarians argue for the idea of a *comparative clause* as a species of *subordinate clause*, alongside *relative clauses* and *content clauses.*

> Our parents knew their grammar better *than we know it.*
>
> More people attended *than were invited.*

These, apparently, are comparative (relative) clauses.

In a *content* relative clause, the relative clause performs a noun-like role (as subject, object or complement):

> You know that you want it.
>
> That you don't like grammar much is clear from your expression as you read this.
>
> It doesn't seem that the government knows how to govern.

10

The four sentence structures

Subordinate clauses—no matter what kind and no matter how they're made—serve mostly to modify sentences. They qualify, describe, define, explain and except. Sometimes, as we've just seen, they also do the work that nouns do. But that's at the margins. They subordinate one short story to another—the dependent clause to the independent—within the body of a single sentence; they let a writer link two ideas, while highlighting the main one.

But what if you want to keep it simpler? What if you want one sentence per idea? Or what if you want to join two equally important ideas equally in one sentence? Then you turn to the other kinds of sentence. If you think about it—if you remember that a phrase is not a clause, neither subordinate nor main—there are only four kinds of declarative sentence you can make. And here they are.

THE SIMPLE SENTENCE

A simple sentence is one independent clause. It may include some phrases, but it can't include a subordinate clause. As soon as it does, it stops being simple.

Simple sentences differ in length—depending, largely, on how many phrases they include. But there's a limit to how far you can stretch one.

Here are a few. (The first contains four prepositional phrases).

> Ernest Hemingway writes in the bedroom of his house in the Havana suburb of San Francisco de Paula. (George Plimpton)
>
> A sensible question is neither a delight nor an annoyance. (Ernest Hemingway)
>
> But paradise is only herself for minutes at a time.
>
> I flew to the island, bussed to the park and stayed there two weeks writing.
>
> A simple sentence is one independent clause.

THE COMPOUND SENTENCE

A compound sentence joins two or more main clauses, and it uses a coordinating conjunction (mostly, *and* or *but*) or a semicolon to do it. What I've just written, of course, is an example. Here are some more:

> Once upon a time there were four little Rabbits, and their names were Flopsy, Mopsy, Cotton-tail, and Peter. (Beatrix Potter)
>
> Every village has its rhythm, and every year Templeton's was the same. (Lauren Groff)
>
> The Prime Minister sat in his red chair, and he cleared his throat and began to speak.
>
> The earth was without form, and void; and darkness was on the face of the deep. (Genesis)
>
> We all do no end of feeling, and we mistake it for thinking. (Mark Twain)

When you string more than two independent clauses together, you make a run-on (or freight-train) sentence, like this:

> She walked out onto the deck in the dark, and she heard the waves of the North Pacific susurrate upon the shore, and she smelled salt and coal-smoke and oil on the breeze, and she knew that she would stay here

till the end.

> He crawled to the car, and he reached his hand in the open door, and he felt about this way and that, and his fingers met the waxy fingers of the dead man lying there, and in those fingers he found the banknotes, stiff with blood.

Where a conjunction joins the clauses, it generally takes a comma in front of it, as in all these examples.

Where a conjunctive adverb, such as *however* or *consequently*, does the job, it calls for something a little stronger—a semicolon—in front of it. As ever, it wants a comma at its tail:

> Coffee likes heat, regular rain and good drainage; consequently, it prospers on the slopes of volcanic mountains in the tropics.
>
> I have always liked the kind of country cattle like; nevertheless, Windorah, some of the best cattle country on earth in its season, was a stretch.
>
> We find the defendant guilty of rape and grievous bodily harm; however, we find him not guilty of murder.

When the link is paratactic—that is, a semicolon joins the clauses—the semicolon does the work alone.

> The crickets thrummed beneath the trees; the frogs started up along the river; the currawongs cried out their names in the dusk.
>
> I spent a lot of money on booze, fast cars and women; the rest of it I just wasted. (George Best)

You need punctuation as robust as this to join together and, at the same time, hold apart two word clusters as autonomous as independent clauses. A comma on its own won't do it. Full stops end sentences; commas don't. Stops and semicolons, colons and dashes demarcate two independent clauses; commas serve for lesser grammatical units. When you marry two independent clauses using only the glue of a comma, you make a *comma splice*. You splice two sentences and call them one. It's cheating. Many literary writers, who can be presumed to know what they're doing, use comma splices occasionally. They make foreshortened compounds; for example:

> My mother died when I was two, my father was a silent and difficult man.
>
> She came with one man, she left with another.
>
> That's not writing, that's typing.
>
> Winter was mild, spring was late, summer was colder than anyone could remember.

But it is never necessary to splice your sentences; at best, it's a gentle offence, committed for a slight effect; at worst, it's just sloppy.

> We played well, we just kept fighting hard till the siren.
>
> I'll send you a copy of the program, it should be back in the next few days.
>
> The whales come up the coast in the winter, in August you'll often see a mother and her calf at play in the harbour.
>
> A comma won't do the trick, you're going to need a semicolon.
>
> I don't know, it seems all right to me.

Conventional grammar would rather you write those sentences like this:

> My mother died when I was two. My father was a silent and difficult man.
>
> She came with one man, and she left with another. OR She came with one man; she left with another.
>
> That's not writing; that's typing.
>
> Winter was mild; spring was late; summer was colder than anyone could remember.

> We played well. We just kept fighting hard till the siren.
>
> I'll send you a copy of the program when it comes back from the printer in the next few days.
>
> The whales come up the coast in the winter; in August you'll often see a mother and her calf at play in the harbour.
>
> A comma won't do the trick; you're going to need a semicolon.
>
> I don't know; it seems all right to me. OR I don't know—it seems all right to me.

THE COMPLEX SENTENCE

You call a sentence *complex* when one of its clauses is subordinated to one, but only one, main clause. (Add a second main clause, and you've got the fourth and final kind of sentence, the *compound-complex*.)

Complex sentences, despite their name, are quite common and straightforward. Like this:

> Although we received nearly seven hundred entries and shortlisted twenty-five outstanding stories, there was always one clear winner.
>
> Mr McGregor was after him in no time, and tried to put his foot upon Peter, who jumped out of a window, upsetting three plants. (Beatrix Potter)
>
> The house, which we discovered in May and moved into in August, stood on the south side of Katoomba, close to the edge of the valley. (Tredinnick 2009)
>
> He's a bold and foolish man who tries to teach the difference between *which* and *that*.
>
> While we're happy to hear you out, we don't plan to make you any promises.

The subordinate clauses might introduce or conclude the sentence; or they might fall in the middle, between the subject of the main clause and its verb.

THE COMPOUND-COMPLEX SENTENCE

So there's one kind of sentence left. It's what you get when you add a second main clause to a complex sentence, or when you add a subordinate clause to a compound. It is the prosaically, if accurately, titled *compound-complex* sentence, and it contains at least one subordinate clause and two main clauses, joined, of course, by a conjunction. The compound-complex is not as strange and rare as you might think.

> Although such sentences seem tricky at first, they are subtle and sophisticated, and they offer the same kind of pleasure as a walk through woods over undulant ground.
>
> He had spent his childhood imagining he'd grow up to be a writer or, perhaps, like his grandfather, a preacher, but, as he grew and neared the end of high school, he shied from his ambition, under the influence of people who might have known better, and enrolled in law school instead.
>
> Hemingway may admit to superstitions of this sort, but he prefers not to talk about them, feeling that whatever value they may have can be talked away. (George Plimpton)
>
> [The music] came across the crowded sidewalk and up through the windows, and even though the organ grinder and the monkey were just across the street, the songs sounded sad and far away, like the music from a dream. (Kate DiCamillo)
>
> He stood, while she smoked, and he saw the future coming down the track.

THE SENTENCE FRAGMENT

If a sentence is an independent clause containing a subject and a finite verb, then a sentence fragment is anything less than that. It is an incompetent sentence. A fragment is a dependent clause with a full stop at the end of it, or it's a subject without a predicate or a predicate without a subject; or it's a phrase or a single word. Full stop. Each of these makes a perfectly respectable *piece* of a sentence; none can be a grammatical sentence by itself.

> Getting the words right.
>
> The boy.
>
> Woke up at six.
>
> While the old regime lasted.
>
> Which gives me an idea.
>
> A line of credit that won't break the bank.
>
> In the beginning.

Technically, fragments are ungrammatical sentences, but they have their place in good, grammatical writing. The trick is to avoid giving the impression you've written them by mistake. If you find one—or if Word finds one for you—ask yourself why you haven't written it up into a legitimate sentence; unless your fragment serves some rhetorical purpose—impact and concision, for instance, make it good. Except in casual emails, notes and text messages, fragments don't belong at work—in a report or board submission, for instance, or in a paper or proposal or letter.

Strictly speaking, most directive sentences (sentences whose verbs used to be said to be in the imperative mood) are fragments. They lack an express subject:

> Romans, go home!
>
> Sleep tight.
>
> Look at me!
>
> Don't worry.
>
> Stop!

But these are looked on as a special case, not as failed sentences. Their subject is presumed; it is the person addressed by the command. Each has all it takes to make it a valid direction, wish or exclamation. So, too, these exclamatives:

> Fantastic!
>
> Congratulations!
>
> Good tidings of comfort and joy!
>
> Bravo!

PART TWO

EVERYDAY METAMORPHOSES

VERBS, NOUNS AND PRONOUNS, AND HOW THEY CHANGE SHAPE; AND A BIT MORE ABOUT DETERMINERS

1

The taxonomy of verbs, nouns and pronouns

Nouns, pronouns and verbs are sometimes called the primary parts of speech; they are all you need if you want to make a sentence. They are the clause-makers—the *who* and the *does* and sometimes the *what*. The other parts of speech, lovely though they are, are less accomplished: they modify, join or signal. They do not, however, name and they do not act, and without naming and acting, or at very least being, you do not have a sentence.

As you might expect, there's more to say about these principal grammatical bits and pieces, and this chapter's where I say it.

Like the fish of the watery parts of the world and the plants and animals of the land, there are different families of noun, pronoun and verb, the three chief orders of the linguistic world. There are seven or eight families of pronoun, for instance, the personal, possessive and relative among them; there are proper nouns and common nouns, concrete nouns and abstract nouns; there are three tenses of verb and four aspects of each tense, making twelve tense forms in all; and there are moods, among the verbs, and voices and all sorts of irregularity. There are taxonomies of the primary parts of speech. And there are morphologies: the primary parts of speech—especially the verbs and pronouns—*change their forms* to indicate what they're up to and *when*.

Compare

> *She* walked out on stage and sang every song *she* knew by *Stephen Sondheim*.

with

> Stephen Sondheim will walk out on stage and sing every song *he* knows by *her*.

My verbs change their form from one version (*walked*, *sang*, *knew*) to the next (*will walk*, *[will] sing*, *knows*) because I've switched from the past tense to the future. The (third person, feminine personal) pronoun *she* changes its shape to *her* in the second, because she stops being the subject of the sentence and becomes the object of the preposition *by* in the modifying phrase *by her*. The (proper) noun *Stephen Sondheim*, however, though it changes its role in the same way, but in reverse, keeps the same shape, as is the way with nouns. Had I used, instead of that noun, the pronoun *he*, it would have appeared as *[by] him* in the first sentence and *he* (as the subject) in the second. For (personal) pronouns change their form as they change their role in a sentence.

These are the everyday metamorphoses this part of the book explores. A taxon, for our purposes, is a group—specifically a part of speech: noun, verb and pronoun, in particular. We're concerned here, at a deeper level than in the last part, with the behavioural characteristics of the most important organisms in a sentence—the nouns, verbs and pronouns. (And because many pronouns put in time as determiners, and because determiners modify nouns, I'll say a bit about determiners, too.) Most of what I write about here you practise without thought or error every time you open your mouth or pick up a pen. But some of it is easy to get wrong, and most of it is important to get right. So here it all is, starting with the verbs.

2
Verbs

It's hard work being a verb. Most verbs have five basic forms (the verb *to be* has eight), and verbs change form more often than you change your mind. A verb changes shape (which is to say spelling and pronunciation) whenever you alter its number (*singular* to *plural*, or vice versa), or person (*I* to *she*), or tense (*present* to *past)*, or voice (*active* to *passive*), or mood (*indicative* to *subjunctive*) or function (*verb* to *modifier*). And sometimes a verb will require another verb (an auxiliary or helper like *to have* or *to be*, *to do* or *to help*, *to try* or *to seem*) to let it do the work the writer intends it to do.

A THE FIVE VERB FORMS

i Plain form

This is the shape any given verb takes in the dictionary; *call*, for example. Verbs also take this form in a number of roles outside the pages of the dictionary. The plain form tells you that the action (calling, in this case) takes place now (in the present tense), habitually or generally. But it only takes this form where the subject is the first or second person personal pronoun in the singular or plural (*I* or *you*; *we* or *you*); or where the subject is a plural noun (say, *birds* or *children*); or where the subject is the personal pronoun in the third person plural (*they*).

> I call you every day.
>
> You call me a friend.
>
> We call ourselves enlightened.

Thirteen blackbirds call from their tree.

They call in unison.

ii –s form

If the subject of the verb *call* is not *I* but *she*, *he* or *it*, the verb takes an *s* at its end:

She calls me every day.

The owl calls from the canopy of the elm.

A verb also takes the *–s form* in the present tense, if its subject is any singular noun (say, *bird*) or another pronoun like *everyone*:

His editor calls every morning to check on his progress.

The postman only calls twice.

Everyone he knows calls him the evening he gets the news.

As in the plain form, the –s form communicates that the action happens now or tends to happen—that is, generally or habitually.

In some verbs—because they are hard to say without an extra syllable—the ending is *es*: *teach* becomes *teaches*. But this distinction, in the present tense, between the first and third person form, holds for every verb, regular or irregular—a quirk of the language.

I write; she writes.

I teach; he teaches.

I throw; she throws.

I hold; she holds.

I party; he parties.

iii Past tense form

Regular verbs add *ed* to their plain form to put themselves in the past tense—the simple or plain past tense. They do this whatever the person, whatever the number. In fact, that pattern or morphology defines a verb as regular; irregular verbs shift their shape in some other way—and there are many patterns of change—when they become past.

> The symptoms *indicate* laryngitis; the symptoms *indicated* grammar-phobia.
>
> He *carries* her bag; he *carried* her bag.
>
> The woman *holds* her breath; the woman *held* her breath. (Irregular verb)
>
> They *buy* their bread at Bristows; they *bought* their bread at Bristows. (Irregular verb)
>
> We *bring* this up each time we *meet*; we *brought* this up each time we *met*. (Irregular verbs)

iv Past participle form

When the verb appears with (and after) the verb *to have* or *to be*, it takes what is called its *past participle* form. With the verb *to have*, in one of its forms, the verb is in one of the *perfect tenses*; with the verb *to be*, in one of its many forms, the voice of the verb is passive.

When the verb is regular, the participle form is the same as the plain past form:

> I called; I have called; I had called; I was called; I will be called; I am called.

Where the verb is irregular, the participle is sometimes also the same as the plain past:

> We taught; we have taught; the children have been taught.

she held; she has held; she has been held.

we thought; we have thought; we had been thought.

But in most irregular verbs, the past participle differs from the plain past form:

I *sing* the song; I *sang* it well; I *have sung* it before; the hymn *was sung* slowly.

I *write* the words; I *wrote* the words; I *had written* the words; the words *had* all *been written* before.

I *forget* the words; I *forgot* the words; I *had forgotten* the words; the words *had* all *been forgotten*.

I *break* the back of it; I *broke* the back of it; I *had broken* the back of it; the back of it *had been broken*.

I *take* the fruit; I *took* the fruit; I *had taken* the fruit; the fruit *had* all *been taken*.

I *sink* the boat; I *sank* the boat; I *have* sunk my boat; the *boat* was sunk.

The verb in its past participle form (without an auxiliary verb) also does service (without any auxiliary verb) as an adjective:

fallen pears, risen sun, elected government, chosen partner, forgotten language, ill-mannered man, targeted spending, abandoned mine, admired bureaucrat, defrocked priest, well-written book, closed book.

I looked in Part One at nonfinite clauses. Each such clause begins with a participle but mostly does without the subject of the verb or the auxiliary element:

The highway follows the path *taken by the first explorers.*

Ignored in her homeland, she went into exile to find recognition and found it at once.

His first book, *read by most of us at school*, is the one he likes least and wishes least to be remembered by.

The name *participle* denotes this ability of the verb, in this form, to part company with its helper.

v Present participle form

This is the verb in its plain form plus *ing*. It combines with the verb *to be* to make the *continuous form* of the verb (past, present and future): *is calling*, *was calling*, *will be calling*. It modifies nouns (without any auxiliary verb): *writing room*, *turning point*, *looking glass*, *swimming pool*. At school, I called it a *gerundive*, in this form, to distinguish it from the *gerund,* where the present participle serves as a noun: I admired her *writing*; I watched his *swimming*; she changed her way of *talking*; they had talked about *separating*. But I don't see that distinction flagged in the literature; maybe the *gerundive* has fallen out of fashion. In any event, that use of the preposition—as a noun—is not what we're talking about here.

The present participle can also, like the past participle, open nonfinite clauses:

> *Running here among these selfsame rocks since the beginning of the Tertiary*, the river is ancient by any measure.
>
> *Thinking on her feet*, she paused and asked him if he knew a better way to find the truth.

Here are some more examples of the present participle, linking with the verb *to be*, to express continuing action:

> The Australian dollar is buying ninety-six US cents.
>
> The commission will be filing in court today a statement of claim alleging breaches by the company of seventy-six provisions of the Corporations Code.
>
> Here's looking at you!
>
> She was warming slowly to the idea of him.

(And the eight forms of the verb *to be? Am, are, is* (present); *was, were* (past); *being, been* (participles); and *be* (infinitive).)

B TRANSITIVE AND INTRANSITIVE VERBS

I dealt with this distinction earlier, when I outlined the five canonical clauses. Some verbs carry no action to an object:

> This kind of thing *happened* often.
>
> That was when she first *appeared*.
>
> And then she up and *died*.
>
> We *fought* like crazy.

In the first three examples, it's not possible to imagine a sentence where the verb takes an object: a person or a thing never happens or appears or dies *someone* or *something*. On the other hand, we might have fought *the disease* or *the neighbours* or *the good fight*. The first three verbs are and will always be intransitive. The last is used intransitively in that sentence, but is not inherently intransitive. Let me give you a few other verbs used both intransitively and transitively (where action passes to an object—a noun or pronoun):

> He writes all day (Int); she writes articles for the local paper (T).
>
> The strategy failed (Int); he failed the test (T).
>
> The play began (Int); Shakespeare begins the play with a memorable line (T).
>
> She cried and cried (Int); he cried tears of joy (T).
>
> And then it stopped (Int); and then it stopped me dead (T).

Ditransitive verbs have a direct and an indirect object; they are doubly transitive:

I gave the chooks their breakfast.

I sent the press the finished book.

I read him a book.

She gave me a kiss.

C REGULAR AND IRREGULAR VERBS

Regular verbs, as I noted, take the suffix *ed* in the past tense; irregular verbs change form in some other way, and some of them change form again in their past participle form.

But regular verbs—slightly under 50 per cent of all verbs in contemporary English—include a number where it's not quite as simple as adding *ed*.

There are some verbs that end in *e*, to which one simply adds *d*:

live becomes *lived*

love becomes *loved*

secure becomes *secured*

change becomes *changed*.

There are some verbs whose final letter gets doubled ahead of the suffix:

travel becomes *travelled*

fulfil becomes *fulfilled*

dim becomes *dimmed*.

US style often does not want the double letter (*traveled*, for example); but the double always seems wanted where to leave it out risks changing the sound: *fulfiled* might sound like full + filed. Neologisms like *focused* cause debate for a time. Usage seems to favour the single *s* for that particular one (though you'll find support for a double *s*, ahead of *ed* or *ing*).

Some words take a *t* instead of *ed*. The suffix makes more or less the same sound in either case; the *t* suffix is probably no more than a variation in spelling that's stuck in some cases. It feels archaic. Strictly these are all irregular verbs, but they're not very irregular.

mean becomes *meant*

sleep becomes *slept*

leap becomes *leapt*

There are relatively few verbs like the first two of these, where an *ed* suffix is not an alternative. And in cases like *leap* and *dream*, *lean* and *spoil*, *learn* and *burn* and *sweep*, most writers would favour adding *ed*, not *t*.

Irregular verbs make up slightly more than half of all verbs in the language—there's English for you. Irregular verbs are defined by what they *do not* do—they do not go *ed* in their past tense forms. Irregular verbs are irregular, though, in many different ways; but each is not irregular in its own way, for there are patterns of morphology among them, and Pam Peters notes fourteen. Let me just note these examples to illustrate the range:

Present	**Past**	**Participle**
read	read	read
send	sent	sent
find	found	found
forget	forgot	forgotten
go	went	gone
drive	drove	driven
give	gave	given
light	lit	lit
wake	woke	woken
lie	lay	lain
swear	swore	sworn
sing	sang	sung

Present	Past	Participle
teach	taught	taught
bring	brought	brought
flee	fled	fled
make	made	made

D NUMBER

A verb is singular or plural, depending on how many subjects perform it. The number of a verb is plural if the subject is a plural noun or pronoun (*books*, *we*); or if the subject is a compound—of two or more nouns (*a hammer and a saw*), of two or more pronouns (*she and I*), of a noun and a pronoun (*Charles and he*), or of two or more phrases (*habitat loss and global warming*):

> A thousand books *crowd* her shelves, NOT A thousand books crowds her shelves.
>
> We are coming to the end of the book, NOT We is coming …
>
> A hammer and a saw lie on the bench, NOT A hammer and a saw lies on the bench.
>
> Habitat loss and global warming threaten the tree kangaroo with extinction, NOT … threatens …

The verb expresses its number by its form; we've seen this above. Often, however, the form doesn't shift from singular to plural: *I go, we go*; *he shot*, *they shot*. The plural form differs markedly in the verb *to be*, and more subtly after nouns and third person pronouns (*she: they*) in the present tense, as my examples demonstrate.

More on this in Part Four (subject–verb agreement).

E AUXILIARY OR HELPER VERBS

Verbs very often do their work in phrases. Auxiliary verbs combine with main verbs to make such phrases as *was helping*, *could hinder*, *don't bother*, *can't bowl*, *ought to try*, *had finished*, *must stop* and *will be relieved*. With the help of the auxiliary, phrases such as these locate the action in a specific tense (this is called *aspect*); they take on a passive voice; they acquire other kinds of meaning to do with orders of obligation (*should*, *must*, *needs to)* and different degrees of potentiality (*can*, *may*, *might*); and they get mood (the *subjunctive* as opposed to the indicative). These subtleties are described as *modalities*, and all of them are beyond the reach of a simple verb alone.

i Primary auxiliaries—have, be, do

I noted earlier, when talking about basic verb forms, the role that *have* and *be* play with participles in making voice and tense. The verb *do* helps express a question:

> Do you like cricket?
>
> Did you have a question?

Do also helps make a negative statement:

> We don't live as slowly as we should.
>
> She didn't deliver her book on time.

Do also helps give emphasis:

> We do so like living here.
>
> But I did get to the church on time.
>
> She never did return.
>
> We do believe in smaller government.

ii Modal auxiliaries

All the other auxiliary verbs modulate the main verb—they ascribe to it degrees of possibility, certainty and compulsion. They partner the verb in its dictionary form:

> *can* change, *could* hurt, *might* help, *may* go, *shall* ensure, *should* write, *will* come, *would* fall, *must* comply.

The words I've italicised are called the *essential modals*, and that's a complete wrap of them. Both *shall* and *will* have history meaning just 'in the future' and something like 'must'. I notice that when I speak, I'm still in the habit of using *shall*, especially in a question construction, to mean 'I will, in the near future'—but only with the first person personal pronouns *I* and *we*. As in *shall we dance?* It looks archaic to me when I write it, but, as I say, I still find myself saying it. Because *shall* still means plain old *will*, it's not your best bet if you mean to convey obligation. Nor is *should*, which implies that it would be the right thing, but not perhaps compulsory. *Must* or some other phrasing will be more reliable. Straight declarative statements in the future tense, or even the plain present, will generally serve. I have a book contract on my desk that says 'you, the Author, grant us, the Publisher, the exclusive right to print, publish, and sell ... the Work in all editions'; and 'you, the Author, agree to deliver the following items'; and 'at its own expense the Publisher will publish and keep the Work in print ...'. That should bind us both.

There is a second class of similar auxiliaries, called by a number of names, including *marginal modals*, which link arms with a main verb in its infinitive (*to print*, *to deliver*), not its dictionary form. Pam Peters lists these:

> be able to, be likely to, be willing to, be supposed to, be obliged to, ought to, dare to, need to, used to, have to.

I wonder about a group of other verbs that frequently get used with the infinitive form of the main verb in what grammarians call the *catenative* construction. Are they not doing the same work as these *marginal modals*? Here are some:

> *want* to go, *try* to help, *manage* to avoid, *seems* to expect, *remember* to call, *helped* to change, *learn* to accept.

I suppose it matters less what we call them than what they are and what they do. Whether or not these verbs and others like them are called auxiliaries, they perform that role in modulating a main verb in a verb phrase.

F VOICE

You give a verb a passive voice when you combine the (*non-modal*) auxiliary verb *to be* with a main verb in its past participle form:

> was elected, will be finished, are astonished, were flooded, was built, had been tested, have been stolen, will have been written, is recommended.

When the verb takes this form, it reverses the flow of the sentence: the subject no longer enacts the verb; the subject receives, or is subject to, the verb.

Active	**Passive**
The voters returned the government.	The government was returned.
We will finish the work.	The work will be finished.
What we saw astonished us.	We were astonished by what we saw.
We recommend ...	It is recommended ...

Writing to excess in the passive voice is a style gaffe, for reasons I spell out in *The Little Red Writing Book*, and I am not the first person to say so. Nor am I the first to point out the uses of the passive voice, among them the way it allows a writer to draw rhetorical attention to the item that is the recipient not the agent of the process described in the verb. But it remains true, I think, that the least legitimate use of the passive voice is far and away the most common—to affect objectivity. Try to ration this function, but for now let's just note the form of the verb in its passive voice—*to be + past participle*—and move on.

The other voice a verb may have is, of course, the active voice. When the voice of the verb is active, the subject, as one would expect, acts; it performs the action expressed in the verb: *the subject acts*; *the river runs*; *the department introduced changes*; *Tom and Geoffrey inspected what was left of the house*.

G MOOD

In Part One, I discussed the now rather marginalised concept of mood. Whether there is an imperative mood, or whether we call it a directive sentence, *Go home* and *Sleep well* and *Look at me* and *Fill in your feedback forms* are all sentences doing similar work, and each of them begins with its verb. We issue orders, not as the Romans did, by altering the form of the verb, but by altering its place in the word order.

Verbs still have subjunctive moods, and when they do, you denote it (some of the time) in how you spell the verb. 'Should any film be censored', I heard a film critic say on radio this morning—'be' betrays the subjunctivity (the hypothesis, in that case) of his verb and sentiment. (He absolutely wasn't suggesting that any film should be, nor was he describing one that had been, nor was he asking a question. 'In the event that a film might get censored,' he was saying.) The subjunctive mood expresses hypothesis or wish or obligation. *God bless you* really means 'May God bless you'; it expresses a hope. The uses that persist in the language articulate something imagined, longed for or hypothesised:

If I *were* you, I'd stop talking now.

If she *were* to become the nation's first woman Governor-General, it wouldn't be a moment too soon.

He *had* better *come* soon; she *had* best *find* herself a new boyfriend.

It's vital he *keep* us briefed.

She accepted this office on condition that she *receive* no salary for it.

If need *be* ...

Come what may ...

Come Friday, I'll be gone.

God *forbid*; heaven *forefend.*

Manners *be* damned.

I propose that the prime minister *stand* down.

One *need* only consider Zimbabwe to bring to mind the vital but brittle consensus upon which democracy depends.

Some of these usages would not suggest themselves to contemporary writers on the page; some are sounding old hat. On the other hand, many of us would utter most of them naturally in speech. As Pam Peters notes, American writing style is more steeped in the subjunctive than Australian style. But many subjunctive forms are still with us; the subjunctive is not dead. It still sounds wrong to write:

If I was you OR If I am you.

One might happily write, though:

I propose that the prime minister stands down OR

I propose that the prime minister should stand down OR

The prime minister should stand down.

The truth is the subjunctive persists, even if some of the modes for expressing it are growing old; it lets us say things we need to say. But a writer needs to guard against, on the one hand, sounding archaic and, on the other, sounding ungrammatical. If you can find another way than the subjunctive expression—and mostly there is one—use it.

By the way, it seems that, while one uses the subjunctive forms in the present tense of such clauses as these—

> She looks at him as if she were sorry; if I were you; if he were to travel;

—one doesn't, any longer, use the subjunctive in the past tense—

> She looked at him as if she was sorry; if I had been you; if he had travelled.

I suppose it stops being quite so subjunctive if it's already happened (*whether it had been you or she*). In other cases, though, the subjunctive remains:

> I proposed that the prime minister stand down.

So, the subjunctive is dead; long live the subjunctive.

The other mood a verb was once said to have is the indicative. But the indicative, in a sense, was the absence of mood. Declarative sentences do indicative work; verbs take conventional forms within them.

See Part One pp 37–40 for a discussion and some examples of sentences in the imperative mood/directive mode.

H TENSE

As I've already noted and as everybody knows, verbs change their form as they change their tense. Sometimes—this is always the case between the plain present and the plain past—the morphology occurs more or less within the confines of the verb itself:

Present	Past
walk	walked
draw	drew
break	broke
bare	bared
bear	bore
hold	held
write	wrote

But the change of tense is often expressed not only by a change of spelling, but with the help of auxiliary verbs *be* or *have* or *will*, or some combination of them.

Tense in English comes past, present and future. But in each tense, we often want to articulate a particular *aspect* of the pastness, presentness or futureness of the action—whether, for instance, it is, was or will be still continuing (at a given point); whether it tends or tended or will tend to happen; and whether an action has or had or will have just finished (when something else in the present tense occurs). For these different aspects of time, English has evolved four *forms* or *families*. This system gives us twelve tense forms.

1 SIMPLE FORM—Indicates habitual or recurring action; uses plain form, plus *will* in future, with suffix *ed* in past.

Present: at present this tends to happen

I talk; she writes; we think; elephants forget; children sing

Past: in the past, this tended to happen

I talked; she wrote; we thought; elephants forgot; children sang

Future: in the future, this will tend to happen

I will talk; she will write; we will think; elephants will forget; children will sing

2 Continuous Form—locates an ongoing action at a precise moment; uses *be* plus *present participle*.

Present continuous: this is happening now

I am talking; she is writing; we are thinking; elephants are forgetting; children are singing

Past continuous: this was happening when …

I was talking; she was writing; we were thinking; elephants were forgetting; children were singing

Future continuous: this will be happening when …

I will be talking; she will be writing; we will be thinking; elephants will be forgetting; children will be singing

3 Perfect Form—describes past action linked to present events; from the Latin *perfectus* (complete); indicates action just completed *when* …

Present perfect: action finished in the near past, and *now* …; *has/have* plus *past participle*

I have talked; she has written; we have thought; elephants have forgotten; children have sung

Past perfect (*plu-perfect*): action finished and *then* (in the past); *had* plus *past participle*

I had talked; she had written; we had thought; elephants had forgotten; children had sung

Future perfect: action will be finished and *then* (in the future); *will have* plus *past participle*

I will have talked; she will have written; we will have thought; elephants will have forgotten; children will have sung

4 Perfect Continuous Form—describes action that has been, or had been, or will have been going on (until now or then), but ends or ended or will end *when* ...

Present perfect continuous: has been or have been plus present participle

I have been talking; she has been writing; we have been thinking; elephants have been forgetting; children have been singing

Past perfect continuous: had been plus present participle

I had been talking; she had been talking; we had been thinking; elephants had been forgetting; children had been singing

Future perfect continuous: will have been plus present participle

I will have been talking; she will have been talking; we will have been thinking; elephants will have been forgetting; children will have been singing

3

Nouns

Nouns *name*. They name *things* we can experience through our senses (actual, *concrete* things) and things we can know only in our minds (*abstractions*—concepts, ideas, processes, qualities); they name things plural and singular; they name things we can count and others we cannot; they name things individual (*child*, *father*, *chair*) and collective (*company*, *flock*, *board*, *team*); they name things common (like *rats* and *gumtrees*, *churches* and *writers*); and they name things proper (like *Redfern* and *Marjorie Barnard*, *the Wingecarribee River* and *Mt Kosciuszko*).

Nouns in English don't change their form much. One spells them other than their dictionary form only

- in the plural (not all of them)
- in the possessive.

Nouns can be subjects, objects, subject complements and appositives.

> *Penny* solved the *mystery*.
>
> *Penny* is my *cousin*.
>
> *Penny*, my *cousin*, solved the *mystery*.
>
> Let me present to you *Penny*, my *cousin*.

Unlike verbs—and unsurprisingly, when you think about it—nouns cannot make other nouns (or pronouns) their objects; nouns interact as compounds (*chookhouse*, *Parliament House*), via prepositions (*the cat on the mat*, *the man in the moon*, *the problem with Mary*, *the cause of the revolution*, *the girl with the flaxen hair*), via conjunctions (*books and readers*, *cats and mats*, *ecology and politics*), and, where the first owns the second, via apostrophe (plus *s*) (*the girl's flaxen hair*, *Alex's paper*, *the prime minister's trousers*).

Nouns appear in all manner of phrases—last *year*, in the *beginning*, all *manner* of *phrases*, from a *friend*, of a *girl*—and they appear by themselves, after definite and indefinite articles, after modifiers of various kinds and ahead of relative clauses:

> *Rain* taught *the rivers* how to run.
>
> *A light rain* fell.
>
> The rain *that taught the rivers how to run* also taught them how to flood.
>
> *No* rain fell for seven years.
>
> It was *a land of little rain*.

A PLURALS

Most nouns take an *s* or *es* suffix to indicate that there's more than one of them (*the plural*). A few have no plural form; a few express the plural in some other way; a few have no singular.

Singular	Plural	Singular	Plural
laptop	laptops	—	auspices
boy	boys	—	genitals
girl	girls	—	belongings
woman	women	breast	breasts
child	children	bread	—
man	men	mathematics	—
lady	ladies	news	—
country	countries	blood	—
house	houses	flood	floods
mouse	mice	sheep	sheep
horse	horses	fish	fish
river	rivers	boot	boots
cow	cows	foot	feet
—	cattle	index	indexes/indices
—	trousers	appendix	appendixes/ appendices
—	clothes	premise (meaning proposition or assumption)	premises
—	pants		
—	premises (meaning dwelling)		

B POSSESSIVES

Generally, nouns change their form in the genitive—in the possessive. They get an apostrophe at their end, and generally an *s* as well.

Tom Tom's

bird	bird's
birds	birds'
children	children's
men	men's
company	company's
companies	companies'

I speak at length about the uses of the apostrophe in Part Three.

C CONCRETE NOUNS AND ABSTRACT NOUNS

Nouns include actual things, which exist in the real world and can be engaged with through the senses:

> shed, book, pen, scent, tree, pear, earth, corridor, wound, tear, chair, woman, flood, baby, crib, air, mountain, orange, piano, singer.

These are called concrete or common nouns.

Nouns also express things that have no corporeal form, no actual existence—concepts, ideas, qualities, notions, trends:

> leadership, power, market-forces, love, loss, grief, hope, joy, redemption, business process reengineering, law, justice, monopoly, tyranny, literature, benchmarking, improvement, climax, disappointment, honesty, management, evolution, ecology, economy, politics.

These are called abstract nouns.

The distinction blurs in the middle:

> poem, song, hymn, symphony, legislation, policy, plan, strategy, festival, conference, meeting, leader, memory, desire.

It's hard to say whether a poem is abstract or concrete; the distinction blurs. Is the legislation the words on the paper or the effect they have on behaviour; is memory actual; and likewise, desire? A *leader*, though one might embrace her, is not, in her essence, merely and wholly a leader, in the way a desk lamp is in essence a desk lamp, or a sod, a sod. When one hugs the leader, that is clearly not all one hugs—one hugs also a human being, who may also be your mother or your sister. *Leader* is a title or label, like *manager*. But in the end the distinction hardly matters—not in terms of form, anyway. As a matter of style, the good writer favours the concrete over the abstract; but all these nouns, the abstract and the concrete and the in-between, are good.

D COMMON NOUNS AND PROPER NOUNS

Proper nouns are the only nouns to take initial capitals. They point to unique individual people, places, titled things (such as books and other works of art, regions and office-holders). Proper nouns are meant to be always proper, but sometimes writers make a common noun proper, by capitalising it, within a document. The publishing agreement on my desk, for example, refers to me as *the Author*, my book as *the Work* and the publishing house as *the Publisher*. This is a legal convention, not in any sense necessary, to make absolutely certain that there can be no confusion about whom an otherwise common noun refers to. But outside such a document, *author*, *work* and *publisher* are all common nouns.

Common nouns are supposed to be things that commonly occur—things, at least, that are not unique. Proper nouns are supposed to identify unique individuals, places or entities. Even though there may be more than one person in the world—or in history—called *Mark Tredinnick*, my name is regarded as a proper noun because it identifies an individual, in his individuality. It's the same with geographical entities, like continents, countries, rivers, seas, mountains and so on. But geographical units somewhat less than names of places—*northern Australia*, *southeast Asia, western New South Wales*—are not treated as proper nouns.

Book titles and things like them would always be capitalised; so, too, company names, product names, job titles and so on. But the noun is only proper and the caps are only required if the title is used in full:

abbreviated forms like these don't take caps, having become common nouns again—*the book*, *the company*, *the manager*, *the accountant*, *the legislation*. Though opinion and usage vary, even *the president*, *the queen*, *the prime minister*, *the priest*, *the pope*, aren't proper nouns when so used. On the other hand, *President Bush*, *Queen Gertrude II*, *Prime Minister Rudd*, *Father Brown* and *Pope Pius XII* are titles—and proper nouns.

A good rule of thumb is this: if you can, or do, use an article (*a*, *an* or *the*) in front of the word, it's not a proper noun (by definition), no matter how important it seems to you and no matter what it says on the business card.

E COLLECTIVE NOUNS

Some nouns, though singular themselves, refer to notional or real gatherings of people, other animals, plants, works or ideas. Fowler called them *nouns of multitude*; we call them these days *collective nouns*.

> team, board, company, forest, range, flock, herd, pod, school, class, department, gang, family, couple, quartet, oeuvre, anthology, discography, repertoire, suite, platform, army, month, mob, (police) force, faculty, synod

Grammatically, each one of these nouns is singular; it points to the group or body made up of all those individuals. Although we may have in mind the individuals on the team, the sentence takes its lead from the number of the noun itself—which is singular. Each of these requires a singular verb after it—even in these cases:

> A flock of birds gathers on the pond.
>
> The West Indian team is wearing its alternative pink strip.
>
> This is a range of mountains that runs most of the way along the east coast.
>
> The family doesn't want any publicity; BUT family *members don't* want any publicity.

F COUNT NOUNS AND MASS NOUNS

Most nouns name things that occur either singly or in numbers. These take plural form when there is more than one of them; a numeral in front of them indicates how many there are. A noun that points to a single entity is called a *count noun*. It will change its form in the plural:

> seven little Australians, three children, 3000 books, ten dollars, four strings, two women.

Because they can be many in number—many instances of the same thing—one can have *more* of them (say, *ten little Australians*) or *fewer* (say, *six little Australians*). And the sign near the checkouts should read 'Twelve items or *fewer*', an item being a count noun.

Some nouns refer to things that have mass, not number; these are called—you guessed it—*mass nouns*; and they can be concrete or abstract entities:

> furniture, luck, grief, water, wheat, milk, bread, washing, light, excitement, economics, eternity, wisdom, foliage, biomass, justice.

Mass nouns can't go plural; they don't make sense with numerals in front of them. You can therefore have *less* of (some of) them, *not* fewer.

G CASE

In Latin, my first name would have been *Marcus*. But the form of that noun, my name, would have altered depending on how it was used in the sentence—as subject, object, indirect object, genitive (dative) or vocative:

> *Marcus* entered the forum.
>
> Caesar saw *Marcum* at the baths.
>
> Caesar gave *Marco* the toga.
>
> Claudia didn't think much of *Marci* (that is Mark's) toga.

'*Marco*; come hither!' she cried.

And so it was with all nouns, not only proper nouns. Every noun changed its form according to what is called its *case*. And so it is in many language systems today, but not in English. Except for the genitive form (where nouns take an apostrophe and an *s*), nouns in English don't change form to indicate their case. It might be helpful if they did, but they don't. Some pronouns, on the other hand, those substitute nouns, do. Let's turn to them now.

4

Pronouns

Pronouns stand in for nouns. Contemporary grammar thinks of them as a subclass of nouns. They are like nouns in function but unlike them in a number of other ways. They don't have the same kind of self-sufficiency; they refer to nouns, which name things; to make much sense, they depend on the noun they refer to. Formally, they are also distinguished from nouns in several ways.

- Some pronouns change their form when they are the object of a verb or preposition. (*I* becomes *me*; *who* becomes *whom*; *she* becomes *her*.)
- Most pronouns do not take an apostrophe and an *s* in the possessive form. It may even be true to say that pronouns don't, with a few exceptions, have a genitive form. Some pronouns (the personal pronouns) change their form but do not take an apostrophe in the possessive. *Who* becomes *whose*; *he* becomes *his*; *they* becomes *theirs*. Although this change of form resembles (in sound, if not in form) the way nouns change their form from the accusative to possessive case, the pronouns, you notice, don't get an *apostrophe* in front of their closing *s*, and, unlike nouns, they change their spelling. Perhaps because of these departures from the morphology of nouns, gram-

mar regards the possessive form of personal pronouns (and *who* and *one*) as an *adjective*. Whenever one uses other pronouns possessively, they need to be spelled out as a phrase: not *which's* but *of which* (but also *whose*); not *each's* but *of each*; not *two's* but *of two*; not *this's* but *of this*. On the other hand, one can legitimately write traditional possessives for a number of indefinite and distributive pronouns: *everyone's favourite*, *anyone's guess*, *someone's apostrophe*.

- Pronouns don't take articles (*a*, *the*), adjectives (*blue*, *this*, *my*, *many*), or numbers.
- Nouns in English don't change their form (as they do in Italian, say) nor take a different article to indicate gender. In the third person (singular), the personal pronoun does change its shape to indicate gender (or lack of gender): *he*, *she*, *it*. This causes problems in expressions like *A writer needs to find his/her voice*. I deal with gender and personal pronouns in Part Four.

These sentences employ pronouns for most of the jobs pronouns do.

> *She* saw *him* driving *her* car.
>
> *He* told *her she*'d given *him* permission.
>
> *She* said the car was *hers* and not *his*.
>
> 'But *I* thought [*that*] *it* was *my* car now', he said. 'I thought [that] you meant me to keep it.'
>
> '*This* is mine', she told him. '*I* bought *it* for *myself* last year.'
>
> '*This* is the car *that* Dad used to drive', *he* replied.
>
> '*Who* do *you* think [*that*] *you* are?' *she* said.
>
> '*Each* of *us* has to make *their* own mind up about *that*', he said. '*Everyone* knows *that*.'

There are eight families of pronouns.

A PERSONAL PRONOUNS

The personal pronouns stand in for people, corporate entities and other things already (or soon to be) named or alluded to. They have singular and plural forms, and they distinguish between the *person* of the noun alluded to; specifically they indicate how that person, alluded to in the pronoun, stands in relation to the speaker of the sentence (its *I*). This—not the fact that they allude to human beings (that is, *persons*)—is where the family gets its name. The concept of *person* applies only in this family.

	Singular	**Plural**
First	I	we
Second	you	you
Third	he, she, it	they

i First person—I, we

The first person personal pronoun refers to the *speaker*. If a writer writes *I* or a speaker says it, they mean themselves. Each of us replaces our name with this pronoun. The plural form of the first person personal pronoun—when there are two speakers/writers, a problematic notion—is *we*: how, really, can two people speak the same text at once; and how can the writer presume to know what the 'other' first person thinks? Still, it's a way for a writer to allude to a family or group he or she belongs to and can fairly claim to know something about. It is a handy way for organisations to refer to themselves and their activities—much more personable than constantly repeating the name of the organisation or employing the awkward *it*, which grammar would require.

> I should tell you that we live on an acre in the country.
>
> I came; I saw; I conquered.
>
> ACME Enterprises makes hybrid vehicles; we like to say we're manufacturing the future.

ii Second person—you, you

This is the pronoun the speaker uses to address the listener or reader. The plural of the second personal pronoun (in modern *standard* English) has the same form as the singular. (Vernacular Australian English sometimes uses *youse* for this, as some American dialects use *ya'll*, but grammar recognises neither as correct.) Many other languages have a distinct plural form for the second person personal pronoun; it's an oddity of English that it does not.

> I should tell *you* that we live on an acre in the country.
>
> *You* may have noticed that *you* has no plural form in English.

You is also employed in writing and speech to mean not the person one is notionally addressing, but people generally, including the speaker.

> You have to be careful with pronouns.
>
> You can never go home again.

This is a kind of contemporary replacement for the indefinite personal pronoun *one*, which has fallen from favour these days in Australia and England, but which in a certain kind of quiet, careful prose, still prospers in America.

One is a member of this class of pronouns in function, but it falls outside the categories of *person*, so I'll touch on it again as a member of the *indefinite pronoun family*.

iii Third person—he, she, it, they

The third person refers to nouns that are third parties to this real or imagined dialogue. We use the third person in a sentence for anyone or anything we talk *about* (rather than *to* or *from*—that is, the speaker). *Third parties* they're called in law.

> The first time we walked into the house, we knew we had to have *it*, if

we could afford *it*.

The thornbill flew hard into the window at two o'clock; at three, I could still see *it* breathing hard in the grass; by four *it* had flown away.

Please sign both copies of the contract and return *them* to me for countersignature.

They came; *they* saw; *they* concreted.

Note that in the singular, the third person pronoun varies its form to account for gender. *She* is the form used for girls and women and certain traditionally feminised entities (though this use is not by any means compulsory and looks sexist in some eyes)—ships and countries. As with *he*, the gendered pronoun is also used for higher order animals, such as horses and dogs, and especially pets, or wherever the gender of the animal is reasonably clear to us. I'd like to have used it for my thornbill just now, but I don't really know where to look to be sure. I'm confident, on the other hand, that my hens are *she*s, as was the possum last night in the oak tree carrying her young on her back. Most people don't extend the courtesy to plants, though some (such as *sheoaks*) come male or female.

He is for boys and men and animals whose male gender is certain.

It is for nonhuman, inanimate things, including corporate entities and concepts; *it* is also used for all the other parts of nature whose gender (and nature, often) we don't care about or can't observe.

Every noun, including your own name, operates in a sentence in the third person, and it requires the *–s* form of the verb:

Mark Tredinnick writes poems and eats just about everything.

Puncher & Wattman is a small and vibrant independent publisher.

The silver poplar leans over the roof of the shed.

The department has lost its head.

iv Case of pronouns

Unlike nouns, personal pronouns change their form to indicate their role in the sentence.

	I	You	She	He	It	We	They	Judith	Company	Bird
Subject	I	you	she	he	it	we	they	Judith	company	bird
Object	me	you	her	him	it	us	them	Judith	company	bird
Possessive	my	your	her	his	its	our	their	Judith's	company's	bird's

> I see you. You see me. She loves him. We love the dog; it loves us back. They know Mark; he knows them. My bird has flown. She's found her flock. The hens have found their perch for the night. It was they who first introduced me to her.

Note that grammar treats the possessive form of pronouns as adjectives. I've included them in this table anyway, to make it clear how those forms (the possessive adjectives, which are really the possessive forms of these personal pronouns) come about—and how they stand in relation to the head adjectives they evolve from. Note that none of them takes an *apostrophe plus s* suffix.

B POSSESSIVE PRONOUNS

Each of the personal pronouns forms itself into a possessive that stands on its own in place of a noun (in its possessive form)—rather than working adjectivally with a noun, as is the case for the possessive adjectives I just mentioned.

These possessive pronouns are called *possessive pronouns.*

	Singular	**Plural**
First	mine	ours
Second	yours	yours
Third	his; hers; its	theirs

> The pleasure is all *mine.*

They insisted on giving me *theirs*. (House, car, money ...)

Every book you see on those shelves is *hers*; *mine*, all four thousand of them, are out in the barn.

Ours is the first driveway you come to after the convent.

C REFLEXIVE PRONOUNS

Reflexive pronouns serve when the subject of the verb is also its object:

Henry cut *himself*.

Lucy lay in her cot and talked to *herself*.

We don't know *ourselves* as well as we think we do.

Reflexives also serve as appositives or modifiers, allowing the writer to *emphasise* the subject of the sentence.

I, *myself*, have no objection.

Maree prepared all the food *herself*.

Reflexives exist in each person, singular and plural:

myself, yourself, himself, herself, itself, ourselves, yourselves, themselves.

Oneself is the reflexive version of the indefinite personal pronoun *one*.

In Part Four, I deal with the mistaken use of reflexive pronouns in a case such as 'Please contact myself or my colleagues if you have any further questions'.

D DEMONSTRATIVE PRONOUNS—THIS, THAT, THESE, THOSE

This is what I wanted to do.

This is the place.

I never said *that*.

These were the days, my friends.

Does anyone recognise *those*?

Each of these pronouns is used in those sentences as a subject or object or complement, and when used in that way, it's a pronoun. Each of them can also sit in front of a noun; when that happens, they'll be treated as *demonstrative adjectives* and *determiners* (see below):

I always hoped to own *this* house and do *this* work within it.

These findings lead us to make the following recommendations.

The board undertook to fine *those* players responsible for the violence in the pub after the game.

E INTERROGATIVE PRONOUNS—WHO (WHOM), WHICH, WHAT, WHOSE, WHERE

These pronouns allow one to ask open questions.

Whom will the nation elect on Saturday night?

Which newspaper will be bold enough to challenge the government's record?

What light through yonder window breaks? (Shakespeare 1597)

Whose trousers are these hanging on my line?

Where will you go now?

Who becomes *whom* when it's the object of its clause, as it is in *Whom will the nation elect on Saturday night?* The subject of the interrogative clause is *the nation*; the verb is *will elect*; the object is *whom*—that is, a party yet to be elected.

Like the personal pronouns, *who*, which refers to people (mostly), changes its form from the nominative to the accusative case. As I've noted already in passing, it does this, too, when it functions as a relative pronoun; the other relative pronouns (*which* and *that*), presumably because they don't allude to people (or because no one could work out how to spell them otherwise) do not change their form depending on their case.

F RELATIVE PRONOUNS—WHICH, THAT, WHO (WHOM)

I dealt with these when we were talking about subordinate clauses. *Relative clauses*, introduced by *relative pronouns*, are one of the species of subordinate clause. The relative pronouns are so called because they *relate* words in a clause they begin back to words immediately before; they are a means of deferring some modifying remarks.

Refer to that section for the different modes of relating and the different, overlapping uses of the pronouns *which* and *that*. Note, too, that both *which* and *that* serve as other kinds of pronoun (*which* is interrogative; *that* is demonstrative). *Who* (which also has other functions; we just saw one) stands in for *which* or *that*, when the pronoun refers back to a person. And, as noted, it changes form to *whom*, when it is the object, not the subject of the subordinate clause it opens.

> This is the desk *that* Henryk made.
>
> She is the girl *who* broke my heart.
>
> At last I get to meet this woman, *whom* I first met through her writing thirty years ago.
>
> Flopsy, Mopsy, and Cottontail, who were good little rabbits, ... (Beatrix Potter)
>
> Sam and his mother carried the cakes to the truck *that* was green and drove out into the morning that was white with snow. (Amy Hest)

G INDEFINITE PRONOUNS

There is a family of pronouns that point to people or things whose identity is unknown or uncertain. They, or some of them, are also useful for including many people or things (or indeed none of them) in a broad class.

whoever, everyone, everybody, everything, someone, somebody, something, anyone, anybody, anything, no one, nobody, nothing

One is one of these pronouns, but it is, as I've noted here, a special case—much more like a personal pronoun than any of the rest of these.

These pronouns often occur in a structure that requires a second pronoun—a third person personal pronoun. (This also occurs in structures like 'Every writer must decide what she wants to do about this problem'. More on that in Part Four.) The pronoun traditionally insisted upon has been singular—*he*, *she* or *it*—and until a generation ago, usage favoured the masculine.

Something got into the flowerbed last night and ate its fill.

Everyone knows what we have to do.

Someone needs to give up his/her seat.

Everyone needs to bring her/his hat.

It is no longer acceptable (if it ever was) to blithely favour *he* in instances like the last two—that is, to presume that an indefinite pronoun alludes to a male. Some writers interchange *she* and *he*. Some go for *he/she*, which looks nothing like a word to me, and very ugly. Others rework the sentence to avoid having to choose. And others, still, use the plural form *they*. All options are better than *he*. I speak more about this issue—and the options open to a writer—in Part Four.

Then there are some indefinite pronouns that point to more than one of an indefinite group:

any, some, all.

Any of us might have done it.

Some don't know where to start; some, where to stop.

All out; all change.

Each of these, appearing ahead of a noun, would be treated as a determiner:

Any writer knows writing is hard work.

All roads lead to Sydney.

H DISTRIBUTIVE PRONOUNS—EACH, EITHER, NEITHER, NONE

These pronouns refer to one only—as opposed to every one—of a class or group.

Each of us must choose.

Either of you may go first.

Neither of us had any idea.

None wants less than her due.

Each of them is regarded as making a singular reference—to one or other or not one—of the relevant group. Again, each of these pronouns, except *none*, may modify a noun—*each child*, *either way*, *neither book*—and when it does, it's a determiner.

5

Determiners

Contemporary grammar recognises as a separate part of speech words it calls *determiners*. This is a new name for *articles*; but to *a*, *an* and *the*, grammarians add other words—many of them traditionally seen as pronouns (they still are pronouns in other roles in a sentence) doing adjectival work, and some of them cardinal numbers. Here are some.

Articles	a, an, the
Demonstrative adjectives	this, that, those, these
Possessive adjectives	my, your, her, his, its, our, their

Quantitative adjectives	all, any, another, both, each, either, every, few, fewer, little, many, most, no, neither, other, several
Cardinal numbers	one, two, three, four, five, ten, twenty-seven …

All words in the class do the particular kind of modifying—signalling or identifying—that *articles* do. Think of them all as a special class of modifier, if you like.

Each appears before a noun, which it modifies in this special and rather unimaginative way.

I saw *an* advertisement in *the* paper.

The pope is coming to *the* city for a world youth conference.

These prizes have become a part of *the* literary landscape.

That dog chased *its* tail.

This policy should change *the* way we treat *our* poorest citizens.

Each government appoints new senior bureaucrats.

Neither provision deals squarely with *this* problem; no *other* law covers it *either*.

There are *fewer* people in Wyoming than real estate agents in Colorado.

The department cited *several* reasons for *its* failure to comply—*eleven* reasons, to be precise.

Some of the pronoun–adjective determiners can be thought of as more like *the* and others more like *a/an*.

Definite: the, this, that, those, which, that, all, both

Indefinite: a, an, each, every, few, many, most, much, little, no, several, fewer, more

Sometimes the determiners hunt in small packs. Then they are called determinative phrases—*all seven* cardinals, *my two* daughters, *not many* writers, *hardly any* water, *a few* ideas. The first determiner is then classed the *predeterminer*.

PART THREE

KEEPING THE PIECES APART

THE USES OF PUNCTUATION

1

'Trip 9s'[1]

It's after midnight in the West Wing. President Bartlet and his senior staff are playing poker the way this president likes to play it. Blue cigar smoke and a little sober drinking. A table covered in green felt in a room just off the Oval Office, and a fair bit of money down. They're placing bets. When it comes his turn, Toby Zeigler, the president's communications director, sees the president's five-dollar bet and raises it five. It's the president's turn. They wait.

'Mr President?' pleads C J Cregg, the press secretary.

'It's the strawberry,' says the president, answering the question he put when he laid his bet.

'Do you call the raise, sir?' says Toby Zeigler, with some heat.

1. From the opening scene, 'Trip 9s', of episode 6, 'Mr. Willis of Ohio', from the first season of the television drama series, *The West Wing*. The episode, like most of the first four seasons, was written by Aaron Sorkin. It was directed by Christopher Misiano; it was produced by Aaron Sorkin, Thomas Schlamme and John Wells (for John Wells Productions); and it aired originally on 3 November 1999. *The West Wing* was made for and distributed by Warner Bros Entertainment Inc.

'It depends,' says the president.

'It depends on what?' says Josh Lyman, Deputy Chief of Staff.

'There are fourteen punctuation marks in standard English grammar,' says President Bartlet. 'Can someone name them, please?'

The table groans.

'Period,' says C J Cregg, Press Secretary.

'Comma,' calls Josh.

Easy, so far.

'Colon,' says Mandy Hampton, Political Consultant.

'Semicolon,' says Sam Seaborn, the Ishmael of the first few seasons. Toby's deputy.

'Dash,' says Josh.

'Hyphen,' says Sam.

The spin-doctors are coming into their own.

'Ah—apostrophe,' says Leo McGarry, Bartlet's chief of staff, glad to get one.

They stop. 'That's only seven,' says the president, looking pleased with himself. 'There are seven more.'

'Question mark,' says Toby. 'Exclamation point, quotes, parentheses, brackets, braces and ellipsis.'

'Oh, wow,' says Josh, impressed, I guess, at Toby's home run.

'Do you call the raise, *sir*?' says Toby.

This is why some of us watched *The West Wing*, for scenes so tightly written and brilliantly imagined. For high-level political fantasy punctuated thus. The show was secretly (sometimes not so secretly) about writing. It was about rhetoric, good and bad, and how it's made. And the small points that hold the large pieces apart, while joining them also together.

The drama of the scene is the conflict of two brilliant minds, and the point of the scene is the perils of pedantry. But this is a moral tale, and there's a sting in it. The president raises Toby's bet and lays down his 'trip 9s' and wins the table. The pedant—who only *seems* to be stuck in his head—is king. Punctuation, it turns out, matters.

You can bet on it.

2

Different kinds of silence

Punctuation tells a reader how to hear your writing. It helps give your sentences the shape—specifically the rhythm—they had when you heard them in your head. It tells your readers—your listeners—when to pause, and how, and how long. And it tells them this so that they might hear the thing the way you thought it. Punctuation—which is those fourteen (some would say fifteen) points, those small notations between some of the words—scores the rests and dynamics of one's prose. Of one's talking on paper. It makes some sentences sound like statements and some like questions and some like expostulations and some like commands. And it keeps the grammatical pieces of a sentence apart so that together they compose, if you're lucky, an elegant and meaningful whole.

Punctuation helps a sentence say what it means by articulating the syntax on which it is strung—by setting off the grammatical bits that compose the sentence. Punctuation does this by making us pause appropriately—short or long or in-between; abrupt or slick or emphatic; slow or fast or medium—between the items sentences are made of—between the phrases and the clauses, and sometimes between the words. The kind of pause that comes first to mind—it was the first piece of punctuation the president's men and women named—is the *full stop* (or *period*). It's the longest, hardest kind of pause, the kind that keeps successive sentences apart. Another kind of pause is articulated by a semicolon; another still, by a comma.

'A comma is a breath' some of us are taught. Well-placed commas—and most of the other marks, too—let a reader take a breath where the writer, if he were speaking the sentence, would take one, too. But a writer mustn't take a breath just anywhere. It truncates meaning; it throws dummies. Don't use a comma just because the thing is running long and you are running out of puff. Breathe only between the grammatical pieces. Otherwise pieces is all you'll be left with.

The comma as pause has been oversold and under-explained. We need a smarter notion. Punctuation lets a reader rest where we, in the telling would rest, and it tells the reader where and how long to wait. The purpose of the waiting is to notice the relationship between the parts as the reader passes among them; the waiting and the breathing and the noticing expose the structure of the short story piecing itself together around the reader. Punctuation points to the hinges, the joins and the breaks. It tells the listener, through the different kinds of silence it invokes, how to take the sentence's bends.

Punctuation marks off, for instance, the subordinate clause from the main; it tells you when an introduction ends; it encloses parenthetic expressions; it separates words or phrases in a list; it marries the appositive to the subject or object it complements; it ties two main clauses together in a compound; it introduces an explanation or an aside; it brackets definitions and scientific names.

Punctuation helps the words do what they can't without a speaker. Punctuation lets a sentence talk, and it lets the reader hear it, almost as though it were being spoken.

The rest of this chapter is a taxonomy of silences and emphases—a catalogue of punctuation marks, organised as Jed Bartlet's team articulated them. There's more to say, you'll notice, about some than others. About all of them I'd say the guiding aesthetic is *so much and no more*.

Punctuation is less important than grammar. It helps the grammar, if the grammar is good; it helps a reader notice how the logic of a sentence runs—if there's logic there to notice. But no piece of punctuation is as significant as the right word and the right clause in the right place. Often there are options—a colon or a dash; a semicolon or a comma, for instance, or a comma or no comma at all—all of them open, each of them *right*. (Some we've seen already. You can use a semicolon or the comma plus a conjunction to build a compound sentence; or you can start the second main clause with a capital—with or without the conjunction—turning it thus into a new sentence.)

Some writers want punctuation at every turn; others want none, if they can get away with it. Style and prejudice (call it taste, if you like) enter into it, and very little in the etiquettes of punctuation can be said to be starkly wrong or right. Much can be said, though, about better and worse. And that's how I mean what follows, in which I describe the places it has long been felt that punctuation of one particular sort or another helps a sentence along. It'd be worth knowing those places and these markings, so that you could make your minimal and maximal punctuation choices wisely and consistently.

But don't get stuck; there's normally more than one good way—normally more than two. Beware of punctuation pedantry. Punctuation's there to help, as long as you put it where it belongs. Use it when and where it helps; use something else, or nothing at all, when it doesn't. Rather than debate the comma or the dash, avoid it. Write the sentence another way.

3

The full stop (.)

C J Cregg, like a good Ohio girl, called this one the *period*. It's right that this was the first piece of punctuation the team named; we use it more than any other. Every sentence (unless it's an exclamation, a command or a question) needs one, even if the sentence is a fragment. To announce its end. That's what full stops do.

In British idiom, by the way, the full stop is the *full point*.

I've used six so far under this heading (and six commas, I notice).

If I'd been writing in North America, I'd have been up to eight stops; it would have been *C. J. Cregg*, illustrating a second use of the stop—in abbreviations.

In Australia, it is already a long time since it was conventional, let alone obligatory, to use stops in *C. J.*—an abbreviation for *Claudia Jean*. Here, *C J* would be entirely and universally acceptable; one needn't, any longer, use stops between the initials of a person's name (*C J Cregg, J R R Tolkien, W H Auden, A S Byatt*).

US style, as advocated by *The Chicago Manual of Style*, still generally favours the use of stops, not only for initials, but for all abbreviations, upper case and lower, including acronyms and contractions: *C. J. Cregg, G.M.C., A.B.C., Dr., e.g., mgr., incl., etc.* At North Epping Primary School in the late 1960s, I learned the standard British distinction between *contractions*, such as *Dr, Rd, Mrs* and *Qld* (words from which the middles have been taken), which were not to receive stops, and *abbreviations*, such as *N.S.W., Tas., B.H.P., W. H. Auden, e.g.* and *etc.* (acronyms, initials and foreshortened words, not ending in the final letter of the actual word so abbreviated), which were to receive full stops. Pam Peters notes that practice and also other approaches, which, for instance, drop the stops for contractions (as I used to) and for abbreviations (like *NSW*) where all the letters are capitals, but keep them for abbreviations (like *Tas., Rev., incl.* and *e.g.*) that use any lower case letters. She comments that the simplest and best solution—dropping all full stops in all contractions and abbreviations (from *cd* to *PJs* to *Dr* to *UNSW Press* to *ie*)—is not yet common. That's not my experience.

Nowadays, partly because it's been championed by the Plain English movement and partly because, one suspects, it's easier to manage in a post-grammar age, the full stop has more or less disappeared in all contractions and abbreviations. This is the case in most major newspapers and book publishing houses, in government departments, universities and private firms. It's what I do, and it's what I recommend. If it's not standard yet, it will be very soon. The full stop no longer has a role in abbreviations and contractions.

Outside its use to close sentences, and beyond its now old-hat use in non-words like abbreviations, the full stop is still employed:

- as decimal points (*9.57*, *7.25 per cent*)
- in sums of money (*$5477.78*, *$1.50*)
- in times and (sometimes) dates (*1.45 pm*, *2.01.08*)
- with numbers and letters, used as or in headings (*3. The full stop*, *2.6.1a*)

To go back to sentences: one uses a question mark in *direct questions*:

> Can you name the fourteen marks of punctuation in standard English grammar?
>
> What is your name?
>
> How long have you lived here?

But where the writing asks the question in a declarative sentence—*indirectly*—the full stop returns:

> He asked if we could name the fourteen marks of punctuation in standard English grammar.
>
> She asked me my name.
>
> I told you how long we'd lived here.

4
The comma (,)

The comma is the original pause for breath. It got named second in response to Jed Bartlet's question, and no wonder; it's almost as commonly used as the full stop. Pam Peters thinks it's falling out of use—and she regrets that. I haven't noticed its decline so much as a widespread confusion about where it belongs. A client of mine put it well when she said 'I think my staff believe there's a jar of commas in the corner; they go and get them when they think of it and sprinkle them randomly in their sentences'.

So, I think the problem is not that the comma is dying out, but that it is widely misused (sins of omission as well as commission) and used where another mark (such as a dash or parentheses or a semicolon) would serve better, thus freeing the comma for the narrow range of work it's made for. Too little is known about the other marks, so the comma gets overworked; and too little is known about sentence structure, so the comma gets put in the wrong places.

You use a comma where you would take a pause within a sentence if you were saying it—but not just any pause. It's best to keep the comma for the kinds of pause one takes between clauses and, less commonly, before or after phrases, and between items (words or phrases) in a series. Avoid using commas for which there is only a rhetorical—but no grammatical—reason.

What follows is a list of the grammatical reasons for a comma; these are the occasions when one tends, in speech, to pause without thinking about it, to articulate not only the words and word groups, but also the relationships between them. These are what some of the books call, for that reason, 'The Principal Uses of the Comma'.

A TO SEPARATE ITEMS IN A LIST—THE SERIAL COMMA

i Nouns (and noun phrases)

> I've written this book for writers, grammarians, students and teachers.

In a sentence like this, the comma marks the natural pause between each of the nouns in a series (the objects of the preposition *for*, in this case); really, the comma stands in for *and*. These commas are called *serial commas*. But note how the comma doesn't appear between the last two items. This is an Australian and British convention—instead of a comma between the two final items on a list of more than two nouns or noun phrases, you employ *and*. I notice that people insist, sometimes shrilly, on the necessity of dropping the comma ahead of that final *and*. But, in fact, the convention to drop it, apart from being confined to parts of the British Commonwealth, is not very old or well established. As Pam Peters explains, dropping the last comma in a series isn't mandatory; nor is it always helpful. I'd add that the *and* we feel compelled to put between the last two items isn't compulsory, either. It's conventional because it brings a list to a point of rhetorical closure. But it is nowhere mandated, and many literary writers abandon it. It can sound too neat and bureaucratic in a story.

American practice still favours the final serial comma (in front of the closing *and*); so, for a long time, did Anglo-Australian style.

> Famine, floods, and war had made the villagers weary and untrusting of strangers. (John Muth)
>
> They talked about cat whiskers, the color of the sun, and giving. (John Muth)

The second of John Muth's sentences here shows how the comma is used to demarcate noun phrases.

Even here in Australia, convention these days favours including the final serial comma where it avoids confusion:

> Coffee grows well in Central America, northern Australia, southern Asia and Africa.
>
> Down in the paddock she could see milk cows, a flock of geese, a mob of kangaroos and sheep.

Southern in the first could refer to both *Asia* and *Africa*, although the absence of *and* ahead of *southern Asia* makes it more likely that plain old *Africa* is the final item. Still, the confusion arises: does the writer mean *southern Asia and [southern] Africa* (which would be factually incorrect) or *Africa and southern Asia*? Putting a comma in front of *and* would help; so would changing the word order.

Likewise, in the second example, the writer may mean either a mob of kangaroos and [a mob of] sheep or sheep and a mob of kangaroos. If you meant, say, 'some kangaroos, and a mob of sheep', you'd put the comma in front of *and sheep*.

ii Adjectives and adverbs

Sometimes we use adjectives in a series, too, and when we do, a comma substitutes for *and* between the adjectival items.

> A thick, black, viscous slick spread inexorably from the listing ship.
>
> The woods were lovely, dark, and deep. (Robert Frost)
>
> Coffee beans are the seed that grows inside a bright red berry.
>
> Sage is a robust herbaceous plant.

But not all the adjectives in a series want commas between them. In the second last sentence, I'd say *bright* and *red* make a compound adjective and might be hyphenated. In the last sentence, *herbaceous* makes a compound noun with *plant*, which is why it doesn't seem to need a comma.

Adverbs sometimes come in series too:

> She loved him truly, madly, deeply—not wisely, but too well.

iii String of clauses

Some sentences are made of several clauses strung together; the comma keeps them apart; *and* may link the last two:

> In Cuthbert's family there was Cuthbert's mother, there was Cuthbert's father, there was Cuthbert's grandmother, there was Cuthbert's grandfather, and there was Cuthbert. (Pamela Allen)

This is a kind of run-on sentence—a long kind of compound. Like the comma between words and phrases, the comma here substitutes for *and*.

iv Appositives

One makes a particular kind of list, I suppose, when one sets an appositive word or phrase beside another noun or noun phrase, which the appositive complements. The convention is to use commas to bracket, or a single comma to introduce, the appositive. This time the comma doesn't say *and*; the comma says *who is also* or *whose name is* or *which is*:

> The writer, Michael Ondaatje, comes from Sri Lanka, via England and Canada.
>
> That honour belongs to Joan Didion, his wife.
>
> AWOL, a nonprofit organisation that cares for adolescents who lose their way, was set up by Tom Browne in 1962.
>
> Three monks, Hok, Lok, and Siew, traveled along a mountain road. (John Muth)
>
> ... and with him was a man, an organ grinder, who played music for the people on the street. (Kate DiCamillo)

Dashes either side of *Hok, Lok, and Siew* might work a little better in the last, given the number of commas in the appositive itself. (The spellings and serial comma should tell you this comes from an American book.)

B AFTER INTRODUCTIONS

A subordinate clause that opens a sentence will always need a comma at its tail. If the introductory word cluster is only a phrase, it will still cry out for a comma if it is of any length. But a writer should feel free to drop the comma after a very short introductory phrase. Again, the pause one articulates with the comma makes a reader notice that some words of introduction have closed, and the main event is starting.

> *When I say I lost my father*, I don't mean he actually died. (Lauren Groff) (Introductory clause)
>
> *At the first gesture of morning*, flies began stirring. (Charles Frazier) (Long introductory phrase; to leave out the comma would cause confusion)

Last year we travelled overseas nine times. (Short introductory phrase)

Before this year is over, I would like to have finished and published two more books. (Introductory clause)

Before this year, I had published four books. (Introductory phrase; comma helps marginally)

During the financial year, the agency met all its performance targets. (Introductory phrase; comma optional)

Sometimes, as in this sentence, a small word or phrase opens the sentence and is immediately followed by a comma. Such opening words are usually adverbial conjunctions: *however*, *moreover*, *indeed*, *thus*, *therefore*, *nevertheless*. *Sometimes*, they are adverbs modifying the whole sentence. Or, again, they are phrases like *of course*. Because they modify the whole sentence, while linking it also to the last, they seem to want a pause after them.

Pam Peters provides this nice example of where and why a comma helps after an introduction:

Fourteen months after the rains came to other parts of the Kimberleys.

Fourteen months after, the rains came to other parts of the Kimberleys.

C IN COMPOUND SENTENCES—TO SEPARATE INDEPENDENT CLAUSES LINKED BY A CONJUNCTION

Most times it helps to let a comma fall between the two parts—the two independent clauses—of a compound sentence. Specifically, if you join the two with *and* or *but*, put a comma in front of it.

There's a light dew, and the silvered grass damps his boots on the way to the barn. (Mark Spragg)

She had a heart as well as an eye, and they were sometimes at war. (Wallace Stegner)

To the north, kangaroos bounded as if in fright or glee, and the three of us in the cab knew we could sail on like this for days with no thought of sleep or nourishment. (Barry Lopez)

If a compound sentence has more than two independent clauses, it becomes a run-on sentence, and you should think about marking the start of each new independent clause with a comma before the conjunction.

> But I set out anyway along the gravel road, and I walked through the antique light of morning and its winter shadows past the horses in the fields and the paperbarks and greygums at the foot of the escarpment beside me to Jim's gate, and I unlatched the gate and walked through it, and I closed the gate behind me again and went on down the drive and through the open door of Jim's great green shed, and I found Jim there in the cavernous twilight saddling six horses to lead a party of riders out.

You have some choice with this comma. But generally, it's better to use it than leave it out; it helps a reader notice that the *and* or *but* is joining not two words or two phrases but two whole clauses. Which is a thing a comma's good for. But you can see, perhaps, from the example I've just given (from my own book *The Blue Plateau*) how it helps to add the comma to the conjunctions that separate the *clauses*, while leaving it out where it joins words (*paperbarks and greygums*) and phrases (*the antique light of morning and its winter shadows*; *down the drive and through the open door*).

US style insists more emphatically than Australian or British style on this comma in compound sentences. This may be because compound sentences, especially run-ons, occur more frequently in American letters, being, I think, a characteristic American structure. But the rule is not narrowly American—even if it were, it seems to me to make sense. Sensible style guides in the United States, like one for a literary journal I wrote for recently, suggest using the comma only when the two linked independent clauses are of some length—or one of them is. By that rule, you'd leave the comma out in:

> She entered the room and she sat down.
>
> I have heard your arguments but I am quite unmoved by them.

But you'd include it in these:

> His father had a savings account waiting to be claimed, but Victor needed to find a way to get to Phoenix. (Sherman Alexie)

> We conducted a wide-ranging literature review of the impact of the built environment within schools on the behaviour and performance of students, and we make these recommendations based on the conclusions we drew from that research.

> The team has overcome many obstacles—not only its opponents, but also itself and its demons—to reach the grand final, and we don't intend to lose it.

> She brought him a lunch of cut sandwiches and a cup of tea, and she told him she was leaving.

D TO ENCLOSE PARENTHETIC EXPRESSIONS

Commas enclose expressions, both clauses and longish phrases (such as this one), that fall mid-sentence. Such sentences (and here's another example), at least where the parenthetic expression is a *clause*, are called *convoluted*. They are one of the four clans of *complex* sentences; see chapter two of *The Little Red Writing Book*. The commas indicate where you break into the main clause and where you pick it up again.

> The best way to come to know Paris, unless you're pressed for time, is to walk it.

> His first thought on waking, if you could say it amounted to a thought, was how much more he'd rather stay asleep.

> In the end, one's home land, once included like a member of a family in the reciprocities of life, becomes a thing, an object no longer part of one's moral universe. (Barry Lopez)

> Old Siew, who was the wisest, said, 'Let's find out.' (John Muth)

You wouldn't use actual parentheses to enclose those internal asides, even though they are called, and really are, parenthetic. You wouldn't use parenthesis because you want your reader to read—you want your listener to hear—those words, right then and there, even if *sotto voce*.

Parentheses invite readers to skip the words they enclose. They're good for definitions of various kinds—information you want your reader to know, but not really to *hear*.

The dash, on the other hand, is good for making asides you mean a reader to hear. You'd use it—either side, of course, of the intruding phrase or clause, as here—if you had a number of commas in the sentence already, or if you wanted to make the parenthetic remark stand out. It also tends to advertise the structure of the main clause more clearly.

> The best way to come to know Paris—unless you're pressed for time—is to walk it.
>
> His first thought on waking—if you could say it amounted to a thought—was how much more he'd rather stay asleep.
>
> In the end, one's home land—once included like a member of a family in the reciprocities of life—becomes a thing, an object no longer part of one's moral universe. (Barry Lopez)

Don't forget the closing comma—or dash. The effect is the same as forgetting to close parentheses or quote marks.

E TO SET OFF NONRESTRICTIVE RELATIVE CLAUSES

I looked at the nature of the nonrestrictive relative clause—and how it differs from the restrictive clause—when I discussed relative clauses as one of the forms of subordinate clause above. There I noted the widespread use of *which* for restrictive relative clauses, where really *that* has better pedigree. But everyone agrees that, when you're making a *nonrestrictive* relative clause, *which* (or sometimes *who* and *whom*, *where* and *wherever*, *when* and *whenever*) is the pronoun of choice. Because the nonrestrictive relative clause introduces information that is non-defining—which is to say, *descriptive* or additional—it helps to put a comma in front of the word, mostly *which*, that introduces it. When such a clause occurs mid-sentence, you'll enclose it in commas, because it will then also be a parenthetic expression. When the nonrestrictive relative clause occurs after the main clause, at the end of the sentence, insert a comma at the start of it. Close it with a full stop.

> Today rain fell heavily across the Western District, which had been in drought for seven years.
>
> I turn to the wall, and for a full five minutes I study it and the painting hanging upon it, which the man who worked here before me had painted—probably standing in the very spot I sit writing now.
>
> The roos, which moved into the wooded paddocks along the river in the winter, disappeared when the cattle arrived.
>
> We shall be judged as a nation by how well and how fast we close the gap—which now stretches to seventeen years—between the life expectancy of Indigenous and non-Indigenous Australians.

Sometimes, as in the last sentence in that list, the dash will serve better than the comma.

Earlier (Part One pp 20 and 62, and Part Two p 94), I talked about nonfinite clauses. If I retooled a couple of the *which* clauses in my examples, I'd come up with *painted by the man who worked here before me*; *stretching now to seventeen years*. I guess this means that nonfinite phrases (called, by everyone, for this reason, nonfinite *clauses*) can do the work of nonrestrictive relative clauses sometimes. When they do, they too need commas before, and sometimes after.

> I turn to the wall, and for a full five minutes I study it and the painting hanging upon it, painted by the man who worked here before me, probably standing in the very spot I sit writing now.
>
> We shall be judged as a nation by how well and how fast we close the gap, stretching now to seventeen years, between the life expectancy of Indigenous and non-Indigenous Australians.

And here are a couple of other examples with words other than *which* pressed into service at the front of the nonrestrictive clause.

This is a bad result, however you look at it.

That was the year my father took us to the house under the mountain and above the creek, where I lived out the rest of my childhood.

I turn my collar up and put on gloves and go down to Somdo, where my tent has stored the last sun of the day. (Peter Matthiessen)

F TO SET OFF EXCLAMATIONS, SALUTATIONS AND VOCATIVES

Sleep well, my friend.

Romans, go home!

Ladies and Gentlemen, I present the wonderful Geraldine Turner!

I'm on my way, darling.

Peter, concentrate on the road, please!

Hello, everyone.

Dear Professor Lopez,

Kiss me, Kate.

Oh, for goodness' sake!

Gosh, what a surprise!

The commas in these sentences or phrases serve a set of related purposes; they follow or introduce (sometimes both) words that call someone (*my friend*, *Darling*, *Peter*, in the vocative case), words that exclaim (*gosh*, *oh*), and words that greet or say farewell (*Hi*, *Goodbye*, *Dear Professor Lopez*).

G TO SET OFF DELAYED JOINING WORDS

One needs a comma, too, before a word like *too* or *however* or *either*, appearing at the end of some sentences. Such words (adverbial conjunctions) usually appear first in a sentence, as we saw above. They may also come mid-sentence, when they'll need commas bracketing them. They may also come last:

This applies to children, too.

I don't want to come, either.

It hardly matters, though.

That wouldn't apply to us, of course.

One delays, in such cases, till the end of a clause, a word or phrase that really introduces it—joining and modifying it, at once, from what precedes it.

H TO STAND IN FOR MISSING WORDS IT WOULD BE CLUMSY TO REPEAT

Another specialised use of the very useful comma is to indicate you've left some words out of a sentence, which it would be clumsy to repeat. This is only going to happen in the second half of a sentence, where generally the second half is a clause (introduced by a semicolon) that sets up a contrast with the first:

> Many fiction writers perform their work by trying to execute elaborate plans; others, by sitting down to see what comes their way.

The comma (along with the shorthand *others*) saves the writer repeating *fiction writers perform their work*, as in:

> Many fiction writers perform their work by trying to execute elaborate plans; other *fiction writers perform their work* by sitting down to see what comes their way.

Some writers make do without the comma; but it helps. One more example:

> Thomas arrived by car; Susan, by boat; Margaret, by hot air balloon.

I WITH DIRECT SPEECH

It is still conventional to use a comma to introduce direct speech:

> Old Siew said, 'Let's find out.' (John Muth)

It is also conventional to use the comma to move from direct speech to the words 'she said' or their equivalent, that reintroduce the narrative:

> 'We are making stone soup and we need three round, smooth stones,' said Siew. (John Muth)
>
> 'But today,' said Siew, his face bright as the moon, 'we will show them how to make stone soup.' (John Muth)

Australian style differs from US style somewhat on the question of whether that comma goes inside or outside the closing quote marks. But I'll get to that (under quotation marks later in this part).

And those, my friends, are the uses—and they should be the only uses—of the comma. They are many, but they are not limitless. Put the jar back in the corner.

Finally, a couple of particular *don'ts*.

1 Don't sever your subject from its verb by putting a comma at the end of a long noun phrase (serving as the subject). No one's tempted to stick a comma after the subject, where the subject is short:

> *She* wrote ten books.
>
> *CASA* keeps the airways safe.

But when it gets long, writers often seem to want to take a breath—and seem to want to articulate it with a comma:

> The release of his fifth book in his fiftieth year (1988), changed the way Australians saw their history and themselves.
>
> The price you pay for the kind of freedom we are used to in the west, is the right of every idiot to have his say.
>
> The use of Indigenous signs and symbols as sources of

> inspiration for the architectural design of prisons (in both two- and three-dimensional representation), will help Indigenous people (prisoners, staff and visitors) readily perceive that the staff and the system are sensitive to and aware of Indigenous culture.

In both cases, and in every case like them, resist the urge to stop your reader ahead of the verb; a comma there creates two sentence fragments and makes it hard to fathom your meaning.

2 Don't sever the verb from its object. One feels the urge to do this sometimes, where the object is a long series of items, or long in some other way:

> All a writer needs is, a pencil, some paper, a desk to write on, and a few uninterrupted hours four or five days a week.

Which should be:

> All a writer needs is a pencil, some paper, a desk to write on, and a few uninterrupted hours four or five days a week.

Beyond those instances, don't put the comma in any of the many other wrong places on offer. It's frightening how often I see sentences like this:

> My mother always wanted to become a journalist but after she met and married my father, she buried that ambition.

Putting the comma there leaves one good clause—*she buried that ambition*—and this clause-fragment construct—*My mother always wanted to become a journalist but after she met and married my father*. If you want to keep these words, try either of the following:

> My mother always wanted to become a journalist, but, after she met and married my father, she buried that ambition.
>
> My mother always wanted to become a journalist, but after she met and married my father she buried that ambition.

Both of these put the comma in front of the second main clause—*but ... she buried that ambition*. The first also brackets the subordinate clause—*after she met and married my father*. The second doesn't worry about bracketing the subordinate clause; the argument for that usage is that it lets the sentence flow by using two fewer commas.

Whenever you put a comma in a sentence, look either side of it to make sure you haven't created a fragment. A comma in the wrong spot severs a sentence where it needs to flow.

And here's a true parable from Canada about a misplaced comma. A communications company thought this sentence in a contract guaranteed them a clear five-year licence to string their wires over the other party's poles:

> The agreement shall continue in force for a period of five years from the date it is made, and thereafter for successive five-year periods, unless and until terminated by one-year prior notice in writing by either party.

They were shocked when the pole company cancelled the deal after a year and upped the rent. But the court agreed that the clause allowed them to do that, and all because, it said, of the second comma. This story—a comma story—made the front pages of the Canadian papers in 2008. The second comma allowed the clause beginning 'unless and until terminated' to qualify the entire main clause—not just to qualify 'for successive five-year periods', which had been the communication company's intention. The communications company lost a lot of money and blamed the second comma, but the comma wasn't really the problem. The problem was the structure of the sentence; the sentence was overwrought; two were rolled into one, and the second was too compressed. When will lawyers learn to speak plainly? This might have worked:

> The agreement shall continue in force for a period of five years from the date it is made. Thereafter it shall continue in force for successive five-year periods unless and until terminated by one-year prior notice in writing by either party.

A semicolon in place of the first comma would have saved the communications company (whether or not the second comma remains):

> The agreement shall continue in force for a period of five years from the date it is made; thereafter it shall continue in force for successive five-year periods, unless and until terminated by one-year prior notice in writing by either party.

Don't make your commas carry the excess baggage of ill-formed sentences. Even if the lawyers had left all commas out of the original sentence, as sometimes lawyers do, fearing the outcome that befell the communications company, the sentence could have been construed as the courts construed it. But lawyers never did trust the comma.

5

The colon (:)

A colon breaks a sentence to say, *here comes an explanation*. The sentence does not end until the explanation ends. Sometimes what follows is a list; sometimes it's a list of words or phrases; sometimes it's a second main clause. But whatever follows always gets more specific and detailed about a summary you've just attempted in your opening clause. The colon is a way of saying *and* or *in this particular way*.

Whereas the semicolon (see p 153) links two elements (generally, two independent clauses) of equal value, the colon links two elements of *un*equal value. The second explains or elaborates on, even completes, the first.

The word cluster following the colon *need not* be an independent clause, but the word cluster *ahead of the colon must be*. Before we all got computers and discovered bullet points, we'd have written this:

> On his desk lay some books of poetry, his grandfather's tattered bible, three opened dictionaries and the remnants of lunch.

Just because you write some introductory words and follow them with a list, you don't need a colon in the middle. In fact, it's wrong, really, to stick anything—a comma, a dash, a colon—between the verb and its object; *lay* is the sentence's verb, and the rest of the sentence is its extended object. It probably wouldn't (and it shouldn't) occur to most of us, therefore, to write

> On his desk lay: some books of poetry, his grandfather's tattered bible, three opened dictionaries and the remnants of lunch.

It follows that you don't need a colon if you turn that sentence out this way:

> On his desk sat
> - some books of poetry
> - his grandfather's tattered bible
> - three opened dictionaries
> - the remnants of lunch.

Nor, you notice, do you need anything, such as commas or semicolons, to keep the items on the list apart. More of that under 'The semicolon' below.

Here are some more examples of where a colon is rightly excluded.

> The convention gives us the chance to set ourselves some stretch goals,

draft ourselves a mission statement, and hear from some bright people we don't listen to enough.

The convention gives us the chance to

- set ourselves some stretch goals
- draft ourselves a mission statement
- hear from some bright people we don't listen to enough.

Here's a sentence where the colon belongs; the words introducing the list make it an independent clause.

To sell this proposal, we'll have to get commitment from these stakeholders:

- local chambers of commerce
- schools
- churches
- community groups
- local writers and artists
- opinion leaders.

So far, we've looked at sentences in which a colon introduced a list of phrases. But sometimes a colon may give on to a second independent clause. Two independent clauses may be punctuated by a colon if the second amplifies or interprets the first. It's difficult, in practice, to decide between the semicolon and the colon—or sometimes the dash—in such cases.

It was hard to miss the implication: get buy-in from council or forget the idea.

There's really only one thing to do: write a book about it.

Grammar sustains and supports creative expression: without it, one has no bounds to push against and no problem to solve.

The colon is also the right way to introduce a quotation, where the words leading up to it form an independent clause:

Yeats described neatly the distinction between poetics and politics:

> 'Poetry is the quarrel you have with yourself; politics is the quarrel you have with the world.'

You might also use a colon, after an independent clause, to introduce a quotation of several lines.

There are, then, some specialised uses of the colon, outside the scope of the sentence.

- TIME: 6.00 pm; CONDUCTOR: Maestro Brian Castles-Onion; PLACE: Taronga Zoo
- *Isotope: A Journal of Literary Science and Nature Writing*
- Song of Solomon 2:ii; *Hamlet* Act One: iii; *Manoa* 18:2
- 3:1—ratios
- in some referencing systems, a colon separates bibliographic elements, such as the publisher from the place of publication:

> Trask R L 1995. *Language: The Basics*. London: Routledge.

6

The semicolon (;)

The semicolon—poised, as its form should suggest, between the comma and the full stop; tougher than the first, gentler than the second—separates independent clauses of more or less the same weight (and structure) and makes of them a single sentence.

We've already seen it at this work in paratactic compound sentences (see p 82). You could open this book at nearly any page and see how you might use it—or, at least, how I have. Although many writers in Australia seem to have fallen out with the semicolon, I like it. It helps my paragraphs cohere. By letting me make *a single sentence of two closely related independent clauses*—which is its purpose—it organises a longish sequence of sentences, especially in an argument, with subtlety and precision; it gives an exposition shape. It brings order to a congregation of otherwise equivalent statements, marrying two of them more closely to each other than either is to the rest. It gives me another means—beyond a succession of simple sentences, beyond subordination and coordination using conjunctions—of relating my ideas and advancing my story or case.

But it must be said: unlike a comma or a full stop, you can get by *without* a semicolon. You may never feel the need for one; but don't let that be a reason to forget that it's there, and what it's for. The second clause may explain the first; it may express a contrast ('on the other hand', it seems to say); it may describe the next step in a process; it may lay out the consequence or the cause or the significance or the price of the first; it may, sometimes, define the idea articulated in the first; it may make an abstraction concrete or a generality specific. It's a means—and there are others, of course—of expressing the relationship between two (or more) main clauses; it helps a reader find their way; indeed, it helps the writer find her way, through a series of statements amounting, sometimes, to something like a coherent paragraph.

Have you noticed how often, already under this heading, I've had occasion to employ semicolons? It's always possible, of course, I'm laying it on thick; I may even be making a meal of it. But I wanted to show it off, doing what it does. Here are some more examples.

> Many grammar books start with the parts; this one starts with the whole.
>
> Writing grammatically is the shortest way to make unambiguous and elegant sense; it is the surest way to make art with words.
>
> Meanwhile, the anti-land-rights lobby organised itself. Millions of dollars were spent on scare-tactics advertising; membership of the Ku Klux Klan swelled alarmingly; RIGHTS FOR WHITES graffiti graced the breezeblock walls of Alice Springs. (Robyn Davidson)
>
> Then God said, 'Let the waters under the heavens be gathered together in one place, and let the dry land appear'; and it was so. (Genesis)

> Yes, Don Fabrizio had certainly had his worries those last two months; they had come from all directions, like ants making for a dead lizard. (Giuseppe Tomasi di Lampedusa)

Generally, the semicolon serves in place of a conjunction (and a comma) in making such compound sentences. But where you need to emphasise or contrast the second clause, you can add a conjunction (*and* or *but*) after the semicolon; and so it is if the writer wants to introduce the second clause with *consequently* or one of the other adverbial conjunctions (see below for more on them). The example from Genesis above, at least in that translation, demonstrates this usage.

> You can mostly rely on him to hit a top C on cue; but I wouldn't count on it tonight.

Strictly speaking, because a semicolon divides *independent clauses* in the manner of a full stop with P-plates, one should use a semicolon only to splice two fully independent clauses. Not that this fact about the inherent nature of the semicolon has stopped writers, including some as fine as Giuseppe Tomasi di Lampedusa, Virginia Woolf and David Malouf, using semicolons variously as commas, colons and dashes. So I'd have to concede that the semicolon has a history as a sort of all-purpose emphatic pause; but I wouldn't want to advertise or advocate that. With all due respect to those very good writers, I have a feeling it is this loose use of the semicolon that has contributed to its decline. So, if you find yourself using a semicolon ahead of a cluster of words that fall short of sentencehood, try a dash instead, or a comma—or turn the relevant cluster into an independent clause.

> Although everyone in his family and everyone in hers (*especially* in hers) doubted them loudly and her brother even ran a book on how long their union would last, they endured; a man and a woman, who, though no one else could work out why, delighted each other till the end.

Try this, instead, in one of the following ways:

> Although everyone in his family and everyone in hers (*especially* in hers) doubted them loudly and her brother even ran a book on how long their union would last, they endured—a man and a woman, who, though no one else could work out why, delighted each other till the end.
>
> Although everyone in his family and everyone in hers (*especially* in hers) doubted them loudly and her brother even ran a book on how long their union would last, they endured; they remained a man and a woman who, though no one else could work out why, delighted each other till the end.

Here are some others:

> The elephant sneezed; a sneeze so hard that the force of it toppled the elephant onto its back.
>
> She was worn and weary from four long months on treacherous seas; cramped together with quarrelling women and querulous children.

Which would go better like this:

> The elephant sneezed—a sneeze so hard that the force of it toppled the elephant onto its back.
>
> She was worn and weary from four long months on treacherous seas, cramped together with quarrelling women and querulous children.

The semicolon is also your friend where you choose to start a clause with an adverbial conjunction such as *however*, *consequently* or *significantly*, or a phrase like *in this instance*, performing the transitional linking this class of word and phrase is made for. In front of *however*, where it opens a second clause, use a semicolon; after *however*, use a comma.

> Broadly, all economists agree on the meaning of *tax expenditure*; however, there is no universally accepted definition.
>
> (This might be more elegantly put if *however* were deferred: *Broadly,*

> *all economists agree on the meaning of tax expenditure; there is, however, no universally accepted definition.* Or, more simply, try: *Although economists broadly agree on the meaning of tax expenditure, there is no universally accepted definition.*)

> We couldn't afford the space we wanted in the parts of the city we wanted it in; consequently, we looked outside the city and found what we wanted down here.

Outside its primary role—separating two (or more) balanced independent clauses—the semicolon has long served to split subordinate clauses (or long phrases) in a long sentence like this:

> But if, as part of the development, Eridge Park Road were to be resurfaced, especially at the end close to the centre, where the current surface is rough and very noisy; if it were broadened where that's possible; and if this bit of the road, most importantly of all, were to become a 50 kph zone—then the adverse effects of increased traffic flows might be mitigated.

I've used a dash to introduce the main clause, when it finally comes, in that sentence, and I'd suggest it, rather than using another semicolon or a comma, or simply running on, because it highlights the end of the list of subordinate possibilities and introduces the main clause. But you might write the thing the other way round and avoid having to make that call:

> The adverse effects of increased traffic flows might be mitigated if, as part of the development, Eridge Park Road were to be resurfaced, especially at the end close to the centre, where the current surface is rough and very noisy; if the road were broadened, where that's possible; and if this bit of the road, most importantly of all, were to become a 50 kph zone.

Similarly, the semicolon has a long history separating phrases on a list introduced by a colon; this is the purpose the semicolon is almost exclusively used (indeed, overused) for, especially in business and bureaucratic prose, these days. The semicolon has proved useful, because of its extra weight, in demarcating phrases in such series, especially when they're long and when one or more of the elements includes a comma.

> The convention gives us, as a nation, the chance to do three things: set some social, cultural, economic and other stretch-goals; discuss a mission statement that describes and challenges us as a people; and consider the thoughts of our brightest minds, men and women we don't get to hear from often enough.

Don't introduce such lists, by the way, with a semicolon—a frequent error. The colon introduces the list; the semicolon divides the items on it. Don't do this:

> I will begin with the facts; there are two main types of coffee beans used in making coffee.

Because semicolons have form that reaches back, in sentences like this, to the old days before the bullet point really existed, many people now insist on semicolons between the items on a list, introduced by a colon and elaborated as bullet-point items. If you use bullet points, you dismember a sentence in order to display its key phrases visually, each on its own line, each with a bullet point in front of it. I suppose, since bullet-pointing is a matter of design, not syntax, writers can put whatever they like, including nothing at all, between the disarticulated items on their lists. But the stylistic devices involved in bullet point lists—indents, dots and line breaks between the items—make the semicolon unnecessary; its role is performed, in other words—and more emphatically—by those devices. Indeed, since the bullet point list depends, for its efficacy, upon the cleanness of its appearance on the page, the use of semicolons clutters it.

So, drop the semicolons between items in bullet-point lists. They're redundant and inelegant.

> The convention gives us, as a nation, the chance to do three things:

- set some social, cultural, economic and other stretch goals
- write together a mission statement that describes and challenges us as a people
- consider the thoughts of our brightest minds.

If they run much longer, especially if you start needing a second sentence to express your thought—start again. You're no longer writing a disarticulated sentence; you're writing a paragraph. Instead, make each item a sentence (or more), and use the bullet point, if you still want it, to highlight where each begins. You may also want to write a sentence introducing the bullet points—something like: *These are the reasons the nation needs a 2020 vision day*. And end that sentence with a full stop, otherwise it doesn't end till the list ends.

7

The dash (—)

The dash suffers a bad press. Though good writers love it, less confident writers use it shamefacedly, as though it were illegitimate, to string jottings into something resembling a sentence. The truth is the dash is an old and honourable piece of punctuation as legitimate as the comma, and something like it in function.

Speechwriters love the dash. It lets them introduce a pause at once emphatic and casual—the way one does in conversation. Read the Gettysburg address, and count the dashes in that careful, shapely piece of prose. Read nearly any well-written and well-edited work of literature, and discover the dash at its elegant work. Think of Winston Churchill leaning over Anthony Eden's shoulder at a speech Eden was about to deliver, and intoning: *It won't wash, Anthony—it hasn't enough dashes*. Or words to that effect.

The dash—to put it formally—is a mark of separation stronger than a comma, less formal than a colon and more relaxed than parentheses.

You use it *on its own* to introduce an explanatory kind of aside that runs to the end of the sentence:

> It lets a writer introduce a pause at once emphatic and casual—the way one does in conversation.

> Many of you will be here because you know and love Patrick White's work—possibly more than I do.

You use a pair of dashes to enclose such an aside—a phrase or clause, sometimes just a word—you want to make mid-sentence. As I've just done, or like this:

> Some years ago—never mind how long precisely—having little or no money in my purse, and nothing particular to interest me on shore, I thought I would sail about a little and see the watery part of the world. (Herman Melville)

> The tunnel wound on and on, going fairly but not quite straight into the side of the hill—The Hill, as all the people for many miles round called it—and many little round doors opened out of it, first on one side and then on another. (J R R Tolkien)

> The butcherbird—named for its skill at dissecting and even skinning the carcasses of its prey—is among the most intelligent and mellifluous of the world's songbirds.

That use of dashes would be called parenthetic. One might use commas, instead; sometimes, parentheses. Sometimes, as in Tolkien's sentence, you might use dashes instead of commas because you have other commas doing their thing in the rest of the sentence; you might even, as he did, want to use a comma or two inside the parenthetic text. The dash works in that case for the same reason it always works—one notices it, and slows without stopping, and eases into the aside. For the dash catches the eye (and ear) faster and longer than the comma. It makes a longer pause. Look at it; see how its long, lean form serves its slowing, linking function.

Parentheses fall, by contrast, like a roadblock. We'll deal with them soon, but keep them mostly for explanations or definitions you don't really want your reader to *hear*; parentheses almost make a footnote of the words they enclose. *Read this later*, they say; *read this if you want to know exactly what I mean or what my authority is*. They add, while also marginalising, some official matter: a scientific name, a citation or a definition.

The colon, as we've seen, introduces an explanation of some kind. The dash sometimes introduces an explanation or summary; but it does wider, looser connecting work, too. It might lead into a qualification or a refinement of terms or even an apology or acknowledgment. It might just offer a pleasant detour—a *divertissement*. It mirrors in speech a habit of good conversationalists, who digress artfully, resuming cleverly where they left off. For these reasons it is said the dash is less formal than the colon and more relaxed than the parenthesis.

> 'Are you writing?' people ask—out of politeness, undoubtedly. And I say, 'Nothing very much'. The truth but not the whole truth—which is that I seem to have lost touch with the place that stories and novels come from. I have no idea why. (William Maxwell)

A dash might introduce a summary of some details listed before it in a sentence:

> I sit in the ebb of winter writing fifty-dollar poems at a thousand-dollar desk—the story of my life.

Or it may, like a colon, lead into such a list:

> The windows gave on to paradise—two horses in a windswept paddock and the sunlight in the rivergums.

A dash, finally, might let you leave a sentence deliberately unfinished. You might want to do this in a story when a character gets interrupted or in an essay when you find yourself unable to say the hard thing you meant to:

> No Tolstoy, no Chekhov, no Elizabeth Bowen, no Keats, no Rilke. One might as well be— (William Maxwell)

The dash is a versatile and efficient mark of punctuation. But like every other piece, its use is not without limits and rules. Learn them, and put it to work for you. Let it trim and, at the same time, relax your prose; let it help you sound like someone talking easily and aptly about something they know.

8

The hyphen (-)

Sticking with the order in which the marks of punctuation suggested themselves to President Bartlet's team, we come to *the* hyphen.

Let me say first the simplest and most useful thing one can say about this contentious little mark—the hyphen joins things together. Outside the specialised use of the hyphen to mark a line-break that falls mid-word, I think it's always true that a hyphen joins words, as well as words and word-like things, within sentences. It makes one word of two. But from that point on, things get tricky.

The hyphen joins two words to make a single (compound) word (like *blue-green* and *labour-intensive* and *long-term*); it also glues prefixes (particles like *non*, *co*, *micro*, *hyper* and *anti*) to whole words to make what are called *complex* words, like *non-residents*, *co-ordinate*, *micro-economic* and *anti-disestablishmentarianism*.

But usage often varies from dictionary to dictionary, country to country, and school of thought to school-of-thought; one doesn't, in other words, always use a hyphen whenever one does those two kinds of joining. Sometimes one congeals the two elements to produce a single word, like *nonfiction*; sometimes, and in different functions within the sentence, the words stay separate, as in *office block* or *short term*.

A quick aside on en-rules and dashes. Just to get a common confusion out of the way—the hyphen, being a compounding mark, is neither the *dash* (—) nor the single-purpose *en-rule* (–). The dash works like a comma or a parenthesis; it *splits* word groups, whereas the hyphen *joins* words (and word-things). The en-rule (–), not listed by Bartlet's crew, stands in for *till* or *to*, expressing a span of time (or place or number) in expressions like these:

1962–63

9.00–12 noon

pp 554–5

Sydney–Hobart

London–Dakhar.

This isn't joining work, either; nor is it the rhetorical splitting work of the dash.

Confusingly, some writers like to use the en-rule (rather than the hyphen) to denote a kind of partnership in cases like this:

Australia–New Zealand Institute. USA–Canada Free Trade Agreement.

Since that's really a species of joining, I'd advocate the hyphen. I mention it because I see it used. A clearer case for the en-rule (or at least a case where the hyphen doesn't seem quite right) might be:

The Association for the Study of Accounting and Ecology–Australia and New Zealand.

But parentheses would be more accurate, or you could reverse the order of the parts:

The ANZ Association for the Study of Accounting and Ecology.

Businesses commonly use either a hyphen or an en-rule or, where the mood takes them, the em-rule for this kind of thing:

> Director–Human Resources
>
> Manager–Marketing and Sales.

In truth, I suspect a comma would be more accurate. Or you could insert the preposition *of*, which is really what the punctuation is trying to replace and why none of it feels quite right.

A dash (also called the em-rule) is not a hyphen either; it has other work to do. Don't use the hyphen with a space on either side of it to simulate a dash. In fact, while I'm at it, none of these similar marks (-, – or —) needs a space either side of it. Put spaces out or your mind; find the right piece of punctuation, and use it, words flush either side.

Here, before we go any further, are some words commonly hyphenated. But few of them are spelled with hyphens by everyone. They include compounds of nearly every part of speech with every other, and they produce:

- compound nouns
- compound verbs
- compound adjectives
- compound adverbs.

> ice-cold, home-made, mid-term, short-cut, two-storey, nine-year-old, sing-off, buy-in, take-over, non-fiction, editor-in-chief, owner-builder, mother-in-law, head-of-state, passer-by, bullet-point, bullet-proof, cold-blooded, co-driver, co-dependency, alcohol-intolerant, post-traumatic, Pre-Cambrian, retro-fit, bright-red, fire-engine

And finally, before this gets ugly, a few general principles:

a When the compound gains broad currency, its hyphen often falls away, leaving a single congealed word. *Co-operate* has become or is becoming *cooperate*; *co-ordinate*, *coordinate*; *micro-economic*, *microeconomic*; *non-fiction*, *nonfiction*; *by-pass*, *bypass*; *over-night*, *overnight*;

post-modern, *postmodern*. All these words were once hyphenated: *overcome*, *forthcoming*, *mainstream*, *downstream*, *shortlist*, *overtime*, *babysit*, *underground*. Sometimes the hyphen drops away to leave compounds spelled as two words: *short term*, *Year 10 [students]*, *total quality management*, *world's best practice*, *income tax*, *capital gains tax*.

b With many, many exceptions, a hyphen suggests the writer hasn't yet found the trimmest way to write the thing. *Time-wise*, *self-test* and *pre-email days* are just sloppy writing.

c Hyphens hold less sway in the United States than in Australian and British usage. Pam Peters puts this down to the influence of the *Oxford Dictionary*. She says Australians are somewhere in between. I'd say we're not sure where we are.

d Some of us like hyphens more than others do. I don't like them much, myself. People like me take every opportunity on offer to drop a hyphen. Other language-users (or is it language users?) take every chance to hyphenate. Taste plays its part. But no one is free to make it up—except perhaps the poet and literary artist, and even then ... Which leads to my next point.

e If in doubt—and you often will be—check a dictionary; check a couple; check the *Style Manual*; check, if such a thing exists, your inhouse (in-house) style guide. Don't trust your colleagues; don't believe your boss. What would they know? Where the various authorities give you a choice, take it. That's where taste comes into it.

f No matter how your taste in hyphens runs, *ration them*. I'm not the only one who finds them ugly and awkward. Don't seek out opportunities to hyphenate; only use them if the dictionary insists. Unless the hyphen really helps to clarify meaning (*English History Teacher*, *Little Penguin Safety Steering Committee*) or to avoid a disconcerting sequence of letters (*antiintellectual*, *deemphasise*), let the hyphen fall away, if it is falling away around you. Let the *latest* dictionary guide you; if it lets you drop a hyphen, drop it at once. And try to write a hyphenated phrase another way to avoid a hyphen completely (not *pre-order your tickets*, but *order your tickets* or *order you tickets in advance*).

g And finally, aim at consistency. If you decide to go with *longterm*, you're going to need to make it *midterm* and *shortterm* (which doesn't look good), and *longhaul*. Hyphenate *co-operate*, and you should hyphenate *co-ordinate*.

Grammarians have noted these general rules of hyphenation. I'll leave the detail—and there's plenty of it— to Pam Peters and others.

a Double-barrelled names are normally hyphenated:

> Andrew Cappie-Woods, Hillary Creighton-Browne, Claude Levi-Strauss, Jean-Louis Forestier, Brian Castles-Onion, Maree-Anne Reid.

But don't hyphenate names whose owners use them unhyphenated (such as Professor Clare Cooper Marcus, Terry Tempest Williams and Senator Hillary Rodham Clinton). Check somewhere; don't presume. In fact, every time you write someone's name, double-check it: it's easy and offensive and unforgivable to misspell someone's name.

b Most modifying compounds (compounds of any variety serving as adjectives) take hyphens when they appear in front of the noun they modify; mostly they lose the hyphen (and get spelled as two words) when they appear after the noun:

> a drought-tolerant plant BUT the plant is drought tolerant.

c Likewise, when the two words are no longer used adjectivally, they very likely lose their hyphen:

I must write and thank you. BUT I must write a thank-you note. OR I must write a thankyou note.

When did the board sign off on it? BUT Have you got sign-off yet.

Is this your first time? BUT First-time riders often need help mounting the horse.

BHP will take over the mine next year. BUT BHP made a hostile takeover [or take-over] offer last week.

d Most *complex words*—made of a prefix plus a word (like *amoral* and *contraband*)—use no hyphen and are set solid:

uncommon, bipartisan, biennial, dissatisfaction, nonconforming, decelerate, decaffeinate, deciduate, unconforming, destabilised, Antichrist, precancerous, deactivate, counterintuitive, renew, rewind, refine, prewar, postwar, postmodern, premeditate, postposition, postproduction, psychosocial, socioeconomic, recover, reintegrate.

But there are many exceptions to this rule.

It seems we feel more comfortable using a hyphen after *ex*, at least where the complex word is new: *ex-wife*, *ex-boss*. *Excommunicate* and *exogenous* and *exaggerate* all do without hyphens. This shows us, I think, that most *complex* words lose their hyphens over time and become one: *preeminent* is fine but, for now, *prebook* is not. Likewise, *email* is now okay; it used to have to be *E-mail*.

Use a hyphen when the prefix ends in the same letter the main word starts with, or if the combination creates a strange or difficult vowel combination. But we seem comfortable, most of the time, with two *e*s (as in *preempt* and *reengineer*) and two *o*s (*cooperative*, *coordinate*):

anti-intellectual, post-traumatic, de-ice, de-escalate, de-emphasise, multi-occupancy.

Use a hyphen when you add a prefix to a numeral, foreign or technical word, neologism or acronym:

> pre-ASIO, post-2000, post-siting, re-cover (to distinguish it from *recover*).

e *Compound verbs* may be hyphenated or unhyphenated (sometimes two words, sometimes one). Some people say that the noun + verb structure normally wants a hyphen (*gift-wrap*, *baby-sit*), while the adverb + verb compounds (*shortlist*, *backtrack*, *doublecheck*, *mainstream, downshift*, *undertake*) normally drop their hyphen and become one word. This may be right, though I have to confess I'd been writing *babysit* as a verb (and *babysitter* as a noun) until I wrote this section of the book. *Fast-track* (adverb + verb) only takes a hyphen because of the double-*t*.

f *Compound adverbs* (two words modifying verbs) don't take hyphens. Generally, you write them as one word:

> downstream, upwind, inland, indoors, outside.

g By contrast, *compound adjectives* (two words modifying nouns) normally take a hyphen.

> tin-eared, evidence-based, all-conquering, reader-oriented, forward-looking, back-stabbing, home-cooked, self-made, two-part, five-storey, two-thirds, five-year-old, black-letter, day-to-day, open-market, user-focused, new-found, old-hat.

But, again, there are many exceptions. Many of these would happily be spelled as two words when they appear after the noun. Other compound adjectives have become one word over time:

> forthcoming, underpaid, overtaxed, longstanding, widespread, mainstream, everlasting, evergreen.

Compound adjectives composed of an adverb and a participle normally make do without hyphens:

> fully fledged, badly damaged, best known, highly esteemed, ill tempered, aesthetically pleasing.

On the other hand, adjective compounds made of the adverb *well* and a participle, are normally hyphenated:

> well-tempered, well-thought-of, well-intentioned, well-oiled, well-liked, well-hung, well-written, well-heeled, well-fed.

Compound adjectives involving numbers and foreign expressions normally do without hyphens and get spelled out:

> Ad hoc, ex post facto, de facto, de jure, haute cuisine.

And certain adjective compounds used tirelessly in managerial or professional settings often go without hyphens:

> twentieth century [literature], tax deductible, equal opportunity, best practice, patient health outcomes.

h *Compound nouns* (two words working as a single noun) vary widely in their hyphenation habits. Some are set solid; some are hyphenated; others stand as two words. Broadly, though, compound nouns (but not the one I've just written) evolve with use from two words to one hyphenated word, to one word: *hay stack* becomes *hay-stack* becomes *haystack*. Pam Peters notes this trend and quickly adds that no one ever agrees, at least for a time, just where evolution has got to.

But, in contradiction of that guiding principle (and its important proviso), Pam Peters then comments that, of all the compounds, the compound nouns are the least likely to be misread without a hyphen; they are therefore the most likely to appear as two separate words.

Depending on where a compound word is in its evolution towards becoming one word, then, and depending on some other considerations (coming next), expect to find a compound noun set as two words:

> desk lamp, government sector, office block, pear tree, swimming pool, chicken run, desert boots, grammar book.

This is all the more likely when the first word in the compound has two syllables or more:

> government sector, chicken run, spectator sport, cricket match, catchment area, river system, landscape painting.

Peters and others point to some trend lines (or is it *trendlines* or *trend-lines*?) among the compound nouns; compound nouns of different kinds (noun + noun, adjective + noun, adverb + verb, for instance) pursue different paths. I'll mention a couple of them here. But I have to tell you I can never keep them in my head.

So my advice is, unless you're absolutely sure—because you've checked it before, discussed it and put it in your stylebook, or because there's an industry convention—*check every compound in a good dictionary*. And be prepared: dictionaries—American, British, Australian and dictionaries within the one idiomatic province—will vary. Make your choice according to your taste, any guiding protocols and, more generally, the principle that hyphens tend to fall away over time. In other words, if you can lose the hyphen, lose it; but don't be too hasty.

Here are the rules I can never keep in my head—the trend lines among the compound nouns.

a Most compound nouns of the *adjective* + *noun* type

black cockatoo, red book, dirty work, lyric poem, fast track, fast food, slow food

(perhaps because they are really just a noun and its modifier) appear as two words, unhyphenated. But:

wildlife, blackcurrant, blackhead, broadband, blackmail.

b Compound nouns of the *adverb* + *verb/verb* + *adverb* variety mostly congeal:

upgrade, throughput, putdown, downfall, download, backdown, backflip, takeover, makeover, writedown.

c Where the compound noun is of the *noun* + *verb/verb* + *noun* type, it all depends. If both words are short, they usually end up as one:

sunshine, catcall, rainfall, windfall, headache, sweepstake, woodcut.

If the verb comes first and is inflected in some way (commonly and *ing*), the words will remain discrete:

racing car, shopping trolley, stepping stone, writing book.

If the inflected (two-syllable) verb comes second, generally the compound noun becomes one word:

horseracing, sightseeing, goldmining, childbearing.

d *Noun* + *noun* compounds commonly get spelled out:

steam engine, motor car, stock market, dairy farm, fountain pen, cricket bat, ticker tape.

But this is a rule honoured as often in the breach as in the observance. Compound nouns made of two nouns often congeal when the second word is a general-purpose noun (like *land*) and relies on the first noun to distinguish it:

> woodland, grassland, snowfield, racetrack, marketplace, chairman, teamwork, homework, bookwork, notebook, trackwork, tracksuit, bandwidth.

Some noun + noun compounds always take hyphens.

- those where the hyphen really means *and*: owner-builder, singer-songwriter, captain-coach, bass-baritone, day-nighter
- those made of several words: church-in-the-round, artist-in-residence, mother-of-pearl, day-to-day, year-to-date
- those made of rhyming (or near-rhyming) words: dilly-dally, hokey-pokey, hocus-pocus, willy-nilly, willy-willy, hugger-mugger, rugger-bugger.

But, look: as I went searching in mind and dictionary for examples to prove each of these rules, I came up with almost as many that disproved it. So, as I say, if in doubt, look about—check your compound word in a dictionary or two; read around among the better books in your field or on your best shelves. If still in doubt, apply commonsense (one word, you see, in this case) and personal taste, and—if you must—the office stylebook! Once you work out how this compound wants you to write it, set up and maintain a stylebook of your own, in which, among other things, you record your preferred spelling. Keep adding to it. And keep checking it. If you're like me, you'll forget some of your preferences from one day or document to the next.

Here is a grab bag of compound words—some hyphenated, some not; some one word, some two—according to the biggest and best Australian dictionaries I can find.

bandwidth, band saw, bandstand, bandwagon, doorbell, desk lamp, earthquake, windstorm, thunderstorm, inpatient, outpatient, post mortem, wellbeing, heart rate, self-ratings, blood pressure, roommate, day-to-day, dayroom, bedroom, dining room, common room, daylight, haystack, headache, headsail, headstone, headwaters, health care, heat sink, heart-throb, heart attack, heartache, heartstrings, full stop, mother-in-law (mothers-in-law), chief justice, attorney general, attorney-at-law, prime minister, passer-by, ambulance trolley, trolleybus, workforce, workplace, workout, office work, out-of-work, horseracing, racehorse, car park, mental nurse, mental-nurse assistants, airlock, aircraft, air mass, air vent, airwaves, air traffic, housekeeping, wicketkeeper, life cycle, lifestyle, life imprisonment, life insurance, lifetime, lifeline, life jacket, life span, livestock, landscape, landslide, land use, steam train, railroad, railway line, diesel engine, fast-track, songline, sightline, peace talks, peacetime, peace movement, peace-offering.

9

The apostrophe (')

The apostrophe arrived in the seventeenth century, and, though its use these days is fundamentally simple, it's troubled us ever since. In the twenty-first century the apostrophe, no matter what the sign-writers insist, has only two uses:

- it marks letters missing in contractions, like *hasn't*, *doesn't*, *we'll* and *she's*
- it indicates, along with the letter *s* (*'s*), the possessive form of nouns: *Phillipa's book*, *the horse's tail*, *Australia's population*.

The apostrophe came into use in English as the language's written forms began to be ordered and codified by lexicographers and scholars. It was put to work marking the place of letters omitted when words were spoken—writing then, as now, was transcribed speech. In that older English, many suffixes (and a few prefixes) from Chaucer's yet older English had begun to erode in speech: *By heaven, my soul is purg'd from grudging hate*, says Rivers in Shakespeare's *Richard III*; *'Tis to be doubted, madam*, says Edmund in *King Lear*; *I'll prove the lie thou speak'st*, says Siward to Macbeth; *But screw your courage to the sticking place, and we'll not fail*, says Lady Macbeth. And those were the spots—those damn'd spots, those particular silences—the apostrophe got to speak on paper.

Traditionally, (singular) nouns in their possessive (*genitive*) form took *es* as a suffix—at their tail—which was pronounced, once, as a full syllable: *Markes book on grammar*. In speech, apparently, that had become contracted to *Marks*, and now the linguists decided to avoid confusion between the singular genitive (*book's*) and the plural (*books*) by putting an apostrophe in the former. So: *the book's many pages* and *all those grammar books*. That apostrophe, of course, only marked a contraction (*book's* for *bookes*); the apostrophe we still use for the genitive form of nouns turns out to be just another apostrophe of contraction.

And so the career of the apostrophe began—standing in for all manner of omitted letters. And among the contractions was the possessive form of nouns. By the end of the nineteenth century it had become standard to mark the possessive of all nouns, singular and plural, with an apostrophe and an *s*, and to extend that usage to descriptions of attribute and connection rather than true possession: *child's play*, *the cloud's colour*, *the traffic's boom*, *the sea's vast extent*, *grammar's particularities*. In other words, the possessive form of the noun (noun + *'s*) came into use wherever one might, alternatively, write *of something*.

THE *GROCERS APOSTROPHE* AND THE CATS PYJAMA'S

Walking back from a meeting just now, I rounded a corner and watched a delivery truck reverse into a tight spot. *Suppliers' of Quality Poultry* it said in red on the side. Another sighting of the grocer's apostrophe. Or should that be *grocers'*? Or *grocers*?

The apostrophe has no history making words plural. Indeed, as we've seen, the (possessive) apostrophe was brought into English to distinguish the singular noun in its possessive form (*writer's*) from the noun in its plural form (*writers*). It would be strange, therefore, to use *'s*—or, indeed, *s'*—to make the plural of a noun. And it would be wrong. But I'd like a dollar or two for every time I've seen (even, I confess, used) what is called, cruelly, the grocers apostrophe. One sees it especially in signage, but also in annual reports, policies and newspapers: *potato's & lettuce's & other vegetable's for sale*; *many department's*; *a dozen egg's*; *ute body's*; *timeless beauty's*; *secret's and mystery's*; *palomino horse's*; *the cats pyjama's*; *two countrie's*; *senior's get in free*; *the star's were shining brightly*. A form I had to fill in yesterday asked me *Are any employee's related to an XYZ employee?* And last Sunday night I saw this item on a concert program: *Two Soliloquy's*.

APOSTROPHES OF POSSESSION

Whenever, at the end of a noun—not to make a plural but to indicate possession—you'd make the *'s*-sound (which comes out more like a *z* than an *s* sometimes), write *'s*:

> Macbeth's wife, Hamlet's father, Henry's cough, the school's problem, the dog's breakfast, the cat's pyjamas, tomorrow's newspaper, the book's pages, the prime minister's message, the boss's daughter, Thomas's whistle, Peter's apostrophes, the children's toys, Shakespeare's will.

S'S

Word has got about that one never puts an apostrophe and an *s* where a noun, including, of course, most plurals, ends in an *s*. You can do it that way if you like, but you get some odd results. The real rule is that where one says *'s*, one writes it. And where one doesn't, one doesn't. One could discover the phonetic or historical reason why some words that end in *s* (or an *s* or *z* sound, like *Bruce* and *moose* and *muse* and *bruise* and *Marx* and *Lopez* and *Ambrose*) sound okay accompanied by a second *s* or *z* sound, if one had the time, but one usually doesn't. Trust your tongue, instead; trust your ear. The exception (allowing one to drop the *s* following an apostrophe) isn't about spelling, as such, or the nature of the possessive noun in question (proper noun or common); it's about pronunciation—whether we are comfortable *saying s's* or not. It's not about how it looks; it's about how it sounds. There are combinations of *s's* and *z's* sounds that don't sit well in our mouths. We don't say those ones, and we don't, therefore, write them.

No one says, and therefore no one writes

> my parents's house, the birds's singing, the countries's agreement, the girls's laughter, my glasses's lenses, the teams' captains.

One place we never want to pronounce two *ss* in a row is where the word, in its plural form, ends in an *s*. So it's a pretty universal rule that one doesn't add the extra *s* to the end of a plural that ends in an *s*. (So, *cricketers' whites* and *voters' wishes* and *hens' teeth,* but *geese's voices* and *women's rights*.) On the other hand, most of us would say, and therefore all of us should write

> Bass's voyages, Banks's discoveries, Ross's losses, Thomas's carriages, the class's proposals, the grass's scent, the sentence's end, the boss's instructions, Jones's voice, James's hopes, Charles's glasses, Barry Lopez's prose, my muse's feet, the bruise's colour, the mice's cheeses, Mrs Marks's grandchildren, this practice's policies.

Many, but not all, of these are people's names. Some of them are plurals; some don't end in *s* but sound as if they do; some are just singular words that end in an *s*-sound. Many guidebooks list a whole lot of tricky rules, and the style guides of the world enumerate the places one drops the final *s* and when one does not. Consult them, if you like. But they make it sound as if it's a matter of complex etiquette, when it's actually a matter of what our mouths are happy saying.

MENS, WOMENS AND CHILDRENS

A few nouns in English do not take an *s* or *es* when they go plural; they change in some other way. *Child* becomes *children*; *woman* becomes *women*; *man* becomes *men*; *mouse* becomes *mice*; *goose* becomes *geese*; *sheep* becomes *sheep*. Watch what you do with your apostrophes (and your *s*s) after those words.

> men's shirts, *not* mens' shirts *or* mens shirts
>
> children's voices, *not* childrens' voices or childrens voices or childrens's voices
>
> women's business, *not* womens' business
>
> the mice's food, *not* the mices food *or* the mices' food

You can get away, by the way, without an apostrophe in some of these, where they're working, often in titles, as descriptive, not owning, possessives:

> Mens room, Childrens Orchestra, Womens Hospital, Fathers Day.

CDs, 4WDs, JPGs, 1970s AND PHDs

You'll see other usages, but it makes no sense to put an apostrophe ahead of an *s* to make a numeral or an acronym plural. Apostrophes have two uses, and neither of them is to make a word plural. One is possession; the other is contraction. When we're talking about these things in the plural only, they don't therefore need an apostrophe:

> 1960s (sixties), DVDs, CDs, JPGs, PDFs, PJs, TVs, GPSs, SUVs, MOs, tens, 1890s.

Keep your acronyms and abbreviations in upper case, and you won't bump into this problem:

> pdfs, pjs, mos, 4wds, phds.

In the 1960s clearly needs no apostrophe; *I like 1960s music* is trickier. You could call *1960s* possessive there, but, if it is, it's the adjectival, not the true ownership, variety. Unless you meant the music of 1960, you could get away without an apostrophe, as in *I like sixties music*. The Australian *Style Manual* would call this an instance of a descriptive noun in the plural, like *visitors* in *visitors book* and *Mothers* in *Mothers Day*. No apostrophe required (and none pronounced).

ST MARYS

It's conventional, though not compulsory, to drop the apostrophe from the names of suburbs and churches and parks and, I guess, buildings named for saints.

> St Lukes, St Marks, St Faecres, Quakers Hill, St Pauls College

Certainly each is an instance of the apostrophe and its *s* working as descriptive, affiliative, not ownership possessives. But only in the case of *Quakers Hill* is the *s* on the end of those nouns because it's plural. So why, if not to make it possessive, is it there at all? It makes no logical sense to drop the apostrophe in these cases, but I need to tell you that it's conventional and allowable. Don't let the pedants tell you you're wrong to want it, though. And check in each case how the college or church or suburb spells its name, itself: do they write it on their website and signage as *The Womens College* or *the Womens College* or *The Women's College*?

Close to where I once lived, there stood an apartment block, put up, by the look of it, in the 1920s, and high up it announced itself in stucco as *St Jame's*. That, of course, is a gaffe by whichever set of apostrophe rules one plays. A gaffe set in concrete.

10

The question mark (?)

One kind of sentence asks a question. It's called the interrogative sentence. It has a particular word order, which I looked at in Part One, and it ends in a question mark. The question mark lets the reader hear the rise in pitch at the end of the interrogative sentence. Are you *following*?

Conventional questions come with a verb first or an interrogative pronoun:

> How are you?
>
> Is this your idea of a joke?
>
> Was that a question?
>
> Have you had enough?
>
> What am I going to do now?

Or, one ends with the questioning words:

> She asked for me, did she?
>
> You were going to ask if you could borrow that, right?
>
> Come and get me when you're ready to go, okay?

Sometimes we put the words in the order of a declarative sentence but inflect it like a question:

> He said that?
>
> She posted that picture on her website?
>
> You want fries with that?

You need a question mark with those if you want your reader to hear the question they ask. Use a question mark wherever your sentence asks a direct question, like any of those above. Use a question mark if someone you quote asks a direct question:

> Jim turned to me and said, 'Did you see that fox?'
>
> 'Do you want me to leave?' she asked.

But leave the question mark out if your sentence asks the question indirectly:

> I asked him if he needed any help.
>
> The boy asked me then where he had been before he came into the world.
>
> The agency asked if we could have the report with them by month's end.

Now and then you might use a question mark, usually inside brackets to express doubt about the spelling or date or some other detail of a thing you need to say:

> Her first book appeared in 1586 (?).
>
> He had three (?) children, none of whom survived childhood.

But it may be more elegant to say 'Her first book appeared around 1586—no one is certain of the date' and 'We think he had three children'.

11

The exclamation mark (!)

Toby Ziegler called this one the *exclamation point*. Not that it really matters, but we call it the *exclamation mark* in Australia.

You're not going to need it often, much less often, for instance, than a question mark. You'd want one, but not every time, with a directive or exclamative sentence.

Don't scare the chooks!

Leave my house, this moment!

Get over it!

Check the colours on that bird!

Well done!

Rise up, my people!

Fire!

The exclamation mark is just to make sure the reader hears the emotion in your voice. But it's never as compulsory as a question mark. Choose the right words, and let them do the talking. The school of thought that favours restraint in writing would suggest you never (or hardly ever) use one. I'm in that school. Less, as ever, is more.

Certainly, I'd avoid—or ration—them in work-based writing of all kinds. Avoid them in directives because there's no point in sounding bossy; avoid them with exclamations in emails and letters because exclamations—of joy or rage or bonhomie—are rarely useful in emails and letters, let alone in policy and board papers. Stick to declarative sentences, humanely and intelligently expressed. Leave your exclamation marks at home.

Someone, from the *let the words do the talking* school, once told me that using an exclamation mark was like laughing at your own jokes.

In a famous episode of *Seinfeld*, Elaine breaks up with a boyfriend because he failed to use an exclamation point when he took down a phone message for her. I think the message was *It's a boy*. (A marginal case, if you ask me.) Elaine then goes on an exclamation-point bender at work. She's a book editor, and in the final scene, her boss, the publisher, calls her in and reads out to her a manuscript she's edited using what one might call a maximal approach to exclamation points. She is appropriately mortified, and I'm not sure she doesn't get the sack. She should have; it's a moral tale.

Here's another example:

Dear Valerie and Robert

This letter is to say how pleased we were to welcome you to our church on Sunday! Although I wasn't at the 8 a.m. service, I have been told by quite a few people that you were there.

I hope you enjoyed the service too! I love hearing Rick Dacey preach. He is so good, and is able to lead us clearly to hear God's word each Sunday! We are enjoying his ministry among us very much.

It is always good to meet new and old friends, and get to know them. I hope you felt welcome and comfortable, and that you will want to come again. I know we will be pleased to see you.

Blessings!

Beware the false allure of the exclamation point. Leave it to the revolutionaries; use it, at home and at work, only in emergencies.

12

Quotation marks (' '; " ")

Quotation marks, also called *inverted commas* and happily shortened to *quote marks* or even *quotes*, are for quoting other people's words verbatim—titles of stories, articles, essays and poems, and a few other analogous items (the smaller pieces of some larger work); a set of words exactly as someone uttered them, in speech or on paper; and dialogue in novels.

Quote marks say *these are not my words; these are* exactly *the words (title, phrase, term of art) someone else used*. The quote marks, I should add, *enclose* the quoted material; the opening quote mark opens the quote, the closing mark closes it.

In his poem 'In Memory of W B Yeats', W H Auden writes, 'for poetry makes nothing happen; it survives/ in the valley of its making …/ a way of happening, a mouth.'

The legislation defines such conduct as 'predatory pricing' and lists penalties including twenty years imprisonment and fines of over a million dollars.

'When I read your book', said Emily, 'I hear your voice.'

Linda Gregg's book *In the Middle Distance* contains her most famous poem, 'The Other Excitement', and the poem contains the phrase, 'the beauty of things/ in the middle distance', which gives the volume its title.

To avoid the 'enforced congregation' effect, where patients cluster in one lounge, the *Australian Health Code* recommends ample choice of places for patients to go during the day.

TECHNICAL TERMS AND SNEER QUOTES

In the last, the quoted phrase is a technical term used in the document referred to. The author might, alternatively, have used italic, as I have done in this book, for such material.

While some writers like to use quote marks to express some irony or other attitude about the words in question, the best style manuals counsel against this. And so would I. If you must draw attention to an expression—I sometimes do it in this book for emphasis—favour *italic* or perhaps **bold**. Keep quotes for when you really need them.

In this example, a letter I wrote to my local council, I was using quotes, against my own advice here, to sneer as well as to be precise (I'm quoting from a Council document). The second purpose is always legitimate, but not the first.

And I'm worried about the precedent Council sets if the centre proceeds—selling off what you are pleased to call 'under-utilised' land to fund projects you tell us we need, when what we need more than anything, in the face of inevitable and increasing population pressures, is to conserve all the green space we can, both within and around the residential areas of the Highlands. 'Under-utilised' land is why we live here and what we need most to defend.

QUOTES AND ITALICS

The last two examples in the list on p 183 refer in italic to the title of the large document from which the writer of the sentence quotes. This is conventional for documents of that order—book titles, large reports, and newspaper and journal titles. See how I've treated the volume of poems, *In the Middle Distance*, in the second last example. The names of the individual poems, though, go in quote marks.

DIALOGUE

Dialogue didn't always have to appear in quotes. It became conventional late in the eighteenth century. While it would be regarded as compulsory in journalism, business and academic writing, and in all the professions, some literary writers regard it as cumbersome. Writers like Tim Winton and Cormac McCarthy abandon it, sometimes using, in the manner of French writers, a dash to introduce speech—or nothing at all. It throws unaccustomed writers at first, but after a while you realise how little we really need it. Most literature, after all, in most language systems for most of human history has got on quite well without quote marks.

QUOTES OR BLOCKS OF QUOTED TEXT

In literature, direct speech, no matter how long it goes on, would be put in quotes (or not, as just discussed). A quotation from a letter or book or some other kind of document might be indented and set, without quotes, in another typeface or in italic or some such variation on the book's typographic norm. In reports, papers, letters and other functional prose, it is conventional to use quote marks for short quotations—of a sentence or two. If the material, whatever it is, runs longer than that, it's customary to drop the quote marks and use a typographic device—

indenting and employing another font—to set the quoted material off from the narrative of the document.

DOUBLES OR SINGLES

Quote marks come single and double: 'single' and "double". Neither has any specialised usage, although certain fields, such as horticulture, will often insist on one or the other for particular jobs. Horticulturalists insist—in papers and magazines—on double quotes, I think, for cultivar names, like the rose "Dolly Parton".

One has a need for two kinds of quote marks, and this is the real reason two kinds exist. The need is illustrated by this example:

> The program tells us that 'John Castles is one of Australia's most brilliant accompanists, and his operatic conducting has been described by the great Sir Richard Hitchcock as "second only to one's own".'

More often than you'd think, you need to deal with words quoted within some words you are quoting. If there weren't a second style of quote marks to turn to, things would get confusing. It doesn't matter whether you use singles for the first level of quote, as I did, or doubles; what matters is that you use the other sort for the second level (the quote within the quote).

But give writers two different styles of quotes to choose from and half will favour one, half the other. It's a matter of taste. Although the Australian *Style Manual* advocates single quotes, most professional writers favour doubles. Most newspapers do, too. Some book publishers (maybe most; certainly mine) use singles; others use doubles. American presses, as well as nearly all journals and newspapers, prefer double quotes—which are pretty close to bible over there. British style guides are divided, and so is British publishing practice.

I'd suggest not getting wedded to one; you're bound to end up writing for an organisation or publisher who favours the one you don't. Nothing turns on it in the end.

It's worth adding that, outside the context of the quote within the quote, it makes no sense—indeed, it will confuse your readers—to differentiate kinds of quoted matter by means of single or double quotes. Some writers use double quotes for sentences quoted, for example, from a scientific paper and single quotes for either technical terms or attitude quotes or both. That's going to get very confusing to use, let alone to read.

Just choose your favourite or your house style quote mark and use it every time you quote, reserving the other kind for quotes within quotes. Use blocks of differentiated type for long quotes; favour italic for technical terms; don't sneer or attempt irony, but if you do, do that in italic, too.

PUNCTUATING AROUND QUOTE MARKS

At the end of the quote. If your own sentence—*the carrier sentence*—ends with the end of the quote, you're going to have to decide whether to put the full stop inside or outside the quote marks. Sometimes the quoted material has not reached its close where you close the quotes—you've not quoted to the end of its sentence. But sometimes the quoted material has also reached its close—it comes to its own full stop—at the closing quotes. And when this happens, you have call for two full stops. No one puts them both in (one inside and one outside the quotes), but editors fight over the possibilities.

1 'For poetry,' wrote Auden, 'makes nothing happen.'
2 In his poem marking the death of the poet W B Yeats, but not of his poetry, Auden calls poetry 'a way of happening, a mouth.'
3 Another poet once wrote, in a similar spirit: 'No one reads poems to learn how to vote.'

I've written each of these the way I like it—from where I sit, the simplest and easiest on the eye and the easiest to remember and repeat. But, partly, I suspect, because this is also the American style, it's not conventional in Australia. Let me take them one by one.

In example 1 above, Auden's words did not, in fact, reach their close where I dropped the closing quotes. His line wasn't finished; nor was his sentence. His poem goes like this:

> For poetry makes nothing happen: it survives
> In the valley of its making where executives
> Would never want to tamper …

Clearly the stop inside my closing quote was not part of the material I quote from. Australian style, as advocated by *The Style Manual*, would, therefore, put the stop outside the quote marks. We can all agree it belongs to the carrier sentence. But there are two interconnected arguments for putting the stop inside—in this case and all cases.

The first is that, for those people who care to stop and notice, punctuation on the line, following punctuation above the line, looks inelegant: '. That's partly a matter of taste, but largely a matter of the science of reading. It might also sound marginal to many readers; and it's unusual to let style trump syntax. Still, I find it compelling.

The second argument is that, since, on balance, that design argument generally holds, one should always abide by it, always enclosing the carrier sentence's closing punctuation within the closing quotes, regardless of all the other many complexities—thus promoting consistency, simplicity and style all at once. One is saved the tussle with subtle distinctions one is forced to engage in otherwise.

But my editors in Australia, except of course in this instance, would have made my first sentence read

> 'For poetry', wrote Auden, 'makes nothing happen'.

Notice they've shifted my first comma, too; I'll get back to that.

In example 2 above, Auden does end at the closing quotes. My sentence ends there, too. Two stops, really; so we choose one. I've chosen Auden's for the reasons I've just articulated. There can no longer be an objection that I've imported a full stop into the quoted material. But, even so, Australian convention wants to dangle the full stop outside the quotes on the ground that one only includes the stop within the closing quotes if the quoted passage *begins and ends* within the quotes. In other words, only if one quotes the entire sentence. I've quoted only the closing line of the second section of Auden's poem, and it's not a sentence in itself. So my editors would make this

> In his poem marking the death of the poet W B Yeats, but not of his poetry, Auden calls poetry 'a way of happening, a mouth'.

In example 3 above, I've quoted an entire sentence (from a poem by another poet). Both schools of thought (and several others) may let me put that full stop inside the closing quotes this time: the stop belongs to the quote and to the carrier sentence, and, the entire sentence is quoted.

But no! I see that even then, Australian style takes the most pedantic approach possible and argues that, since the clause within the quotes follows a colon in the carrier sentence, it is not, in this context, a complete sentence. So, even here, I'd be asked to put the full stop outside the quote marks.

> Another poet once wrote, in a similar spirit: 'No one reads poems to learn how to vote'.

A small fight might also break out if I wrote my carrier sentence this way:

> Another poet once wrote, in a similar spirit, that 'No one reads poems to learn how to vote.'

I think, in this case, US style would rather I take out the capital *N* at the start of the quote; in my experience US editors want you to leave out capitals that would not belong to a quoted word if it were not quoted, but part of the carrier sentence. Australian style would, I believe, favour keeping the capital because that's how the original went.

In summary, the Australian style privileges the integrity of the quoted material over anything else. The downside is that you have to think too hard; the corollary of that is style that is hard for an editor to manage let alone a writer on deadline, let alone a team of writers on deadline; the other corollary is that you end up with stops in different places in text. Most readers won't even notice (an argument in support of each approach, but especially for doing it in the most repeatable and stylish fashion).

All of this creates more heat than light among editors and within organisations of my acquaintance. In the end, it hardly matters, except that everyone is anxious about getting it right. The whole thing becomes another stick for the pedants to hit the rest of us with.

At work, develop a house style and have everyone apply it. Whether it's right or wrong matters less than that it's consistently applied. As a writer, if you have a view about this and it matters to you, push your publisher to do it your way, even if it cuts against their house style. It's your book or poem or essay or story, after all, and your name's on it for forever after.

I'm not going to the barricades over it, but I'd like to change Australian style. It's pedantic and hard to apply. It's silly and it's inelegant.

At the start of the quote. No one can even agree how best to punctuate where the carrier sentence introduces the quote. These are the three options, and none is wrong:

1. In his poem, Auden calls poetry, 'a way of happening, a mouth'.
2. In his poem, Auden calls poetry 'a way of happening, a mouth'.
3. In his poem, Auden calls poetry: 'a way of happening, a mouth'.

The first, using a comma, is the oldest and it's still conventional. The comma doesn't do much, though, when you think about it. For this reason, much contemporary prose leaves it out, as in 2. The third approach, becoming common in the press, seems clumsy by comparison. A colon might be good for introducing a long quote; it might be permissible when the quote is at least an independent clause and the words introducing it also compose an independent clause—those are the rules about colons.

If you have a choice, take the second. Resist the third. Give in to the first if you have no choice or, like me, can't kick the habit. Here's another example, using dialogue:

> Jim turned to him and said, 'I never did know a comma from a colon'.
>
> Jim turned to him and said 'I never did know a comma from a colon'.
>
> Jim turned to him and said: 'I never did know a comma from a colon'.

In the middle of a quote. Sometimes one cuts into the midst of a quote or a piece of dialogue to attribute it to its speaker. I did this in my opening Auden sentence above, and I noted a controversy over my comma placement. Here's what I did:

> 'For poetry,' wrote Auden, 'makes nothing happen.'

See how I break into the quote after its opening two words? Everyone agrees that a comma is needed to mark the break. American style, consistently with its view about closing punctuation, wants the comma inside the closing quotes, even where, as here, the comma belongs to the carrier sentence and not to the quote. Australian style places the comma outside the quotes, as it places the stop at the end outside the closing quotes. Everyone likes the comma that leads a reader back into the quote placed outside (ahead of) the open quote. Here's the sentence in Australian parlance:

> 'For poetry', wrote Auden, 'makes nothing happen'.

And here's another like it:

> 'I never did know', said Jim, turning to his son, 'a comma from a colon'.

Everyone agrees on these, though:

> 'What's your name?' he asked.
>
> 'Go to hell!' she screamed.

That is, punctuation belonging to the quoted passage trumps the comma that belongs to the carrier sentence. Australian style would, like American style, go with a comma inside the quote marks, if it belongs to the quote, as here:

> 'When I first saw you,' she said, 'I knew it wouldn't be the last time'.

If the carrier sentence ends at the equivalent of *she said* (as in the example that follows) but the quoted talking picks up again on the other side of it, you'll need to start the new bit with a cap. If it's a sentence (or more than one), then all styles would place its final full stop (or whatever it ends with) inside the closing quotes:

> 'It's late', she said. 'I'm going home.'

Or you might get this:

> 'Look', she said; 'it doesn't really matter'.

For a few other complexities, I refer you to the *Style Manual* and Pam Peters.

13

Brackets, parentheses, braces ([ ], ( ), { })

Each of these is a different kind of—what most of us would call—bracket. Each sets off, pretty emphatically, a cluster of words, simultaneously drawing attention to and plucking it from the sentence's spotlight. I'll take them in the order Toby rattled them off.

A BRACKETS

Toby mentioned these first on his list not because they are the most important but because they do their most important job within quoted material—and quotes, as you'll recall, were the previous item on the list. By *brackets*, Toby meant what I grew up calling *square brackets [ ]*. Brackets serve only one purpose that's worth knowing about: they let you drop into quoted matter some words—a comment, an explanation, or a word not used in the quote but necessary to make sense of it—or even a single letter.

> The prime minister said, 'I am honoured to call [Senator Obama] a friend'. *What the prime minister actually said was 'I am honoured to call him a friend'.*
>
> *The Australian Safety Standards* require 'fire-extinguishers in every [class] room'. *The standards, in the passage quoted, did not refer expressly to classrooms.*
>
> '[H]e is scattered among a hundred cities', wrote Auden of Yeats. *Auden's poem didn't use a capital* H *for* he.

US editors would, I think, simply add that capital *H* in the last example. They'd argue, and I'd agree with them, that the brackets look cluttered and fussy, and that the needs of the carrier sentence—in this case, for a capital letter to begin it—override the integrity of the quote, where, as here, the change alters nothing material (like the meaning and the wording) in the quote.

The brackets say this wasn't in the original.

Some people use brackets around *sic*. *Sic* is an abbreviation by which the author of the carrier sentence lets us know she understands that the author she quotes has fallen into an error of spelling or grammar, style or politics or something. Don't use *sic*, with or without brackets. The deal is that quoted matter belongs to its author, not to you. If you want to comment on an error, do it in your narrative, outside the quote. More generally, avoid quoting something you have to disparage. It looks like sneering or pomposity.

For every interpolation within your own text—as opposed to quoted material—parentheses will do.

B PARENTHESES ( )

Parentheses, which you might know as *round brackets*, enclose parenthetic remarks—a word, phrase, or clause—within a sentence. Sometimes they even contain an entire sentence, which starts and finishes within the parentheses.

I mentioned them earlier as an alternative to bracketing commas or dashes. In this role, they are the most intrusive mark, and I commented that in my view they're best kept for remarks you really don't need your reader to hear, but need them to know. Dashes enclose conversational asides; commas do the same thing less noticeably and work when the rest of the sentence contains few other commas; parentheses enclose comments that are effectively footnotes. Parentheses are the least literary and the most scientific of the three marks you might make to bracket interpolations. (It may be because they are so unliterary that a certain brand of postmodern poetry has used them frequently—a kind of transgression, a kind of literary sedition, a kind of appropriation from another discourse.) Favour the other two (unless it's something quite scientific you're writing) in about equal measure; keep the parentheses for such things as scientific or technical names, titles, definitions, numbers, page references, cross-references and citations. But it's really a matter of judgment and taste.

> Every year a shocking number of new English language titles (something above 250 000) are published across the world.
>
> Two species of eucalypt (*E. seiberi* and *E. fastigiata*) dominate the edge of the cliffs above the valley.
>
> If I'd stopped to think about it (and I didn't because I wasn't thinking about anything much at the time), I wouldn't have got in the car and I wouldn't have met him and I wouldn't have ended up here.

> For inpatients, these dayrooms can be noisy and over-stimulating; when conflict arises, staff have few 'neutral corners' to send patients to (Barnes 2006; Dvoskin et al. 2002).

> My shed (a four-stand walk through, according to an old dairyman I met along the river) has stood here above the floodplain for over a hundred years.

A writer might put an entire sentence in parentheses in a paragraph as one might put a word cluster in parentheses in a sentence, and for the same reasons. You want to mention the thing, but you want to play it down in the paragraph—it not being quite on message. So I might put these two sentences at the start of a paragraph that goes on to describe how I work in my shed:

> My cowshed has stood here above the floodplain for over a hundred years. (According to an old dairyman I met along the river, it's a four-stand walk-through, which would have milked sixty head twice a day, in its day.)

You put the stop inside the closing parenthesis only if it belongs exclusively, like this one, to the words within the parenthesis. If I rewrote these two sentences as one, as follows, the full stop would go outside the parenthesis, even though the words within it are a full sentence, because, otherwise, all you appear to have finished is the wording within the brackets. A closing parenthesis falls, as I've said, like a roadblock across a sentence; and it more emphatically finishes whatever its twin began (and not the whole sentence).

> My cowshed has stood here above the floodplain for over a hundred years (according to an old dairyman I met along the river, it's a four-stand walk-through, which would have milked sixty head twice a day, in its day).

Unless the passage within the parentheses begins with a capital, don't put a full stop at the end of it (inside the parentheses, I mean). (I just gave you another example, of course, of how it works, and this sentence is another.)

C BRACES { }

Toby Ziegler must know something I don't. I can't think of a single use in text—as opposed to mathematics or design—for braces (otherwise known as *curly brackets*). They are used in linguistics, according to Pam Peters, to 'identify the morphemes of a language'. This may be the thing Toby knew, and I did not. But then he should have mentioned *slash brackets* / / and angle brackets < >, which also function in linguistics. The slash is almost universally used (misused, really), in place of the en-rule (–), to denote the span of a financial year: 2007/08.

14

The ellipsis (...)

The ellipsis lets a reader know you've left some words out of a quote. In your own text, it lets a sentence trail off, leaving something unsayable unsaid. The second function is appropriate only in creative writing or journalism, and I wouldn't go using it there too much unless you want to look like a rank ...

> It rained the first day, and it rained the second day, and day after day for two long weeks it rained on ...

By the way, though it used to be conventional to indicate the full stop, too, if the ellipsis (three dots) ran to the end of the sentence, it's no longer necessary in Australia. Three stops will do the trick wherever the ellipsis falls.

Except, perhaps, to indicate in dialogue or stream of consciousness, how a character keeps losing their train of thought, I wouldn't suggest using the ellipsis for this kind of fade-out.

Keep it for quotes. You may need it there to indicate where you've omitted some—presumably immaterial—words. If the quote is as short as a phrase or clause, you're unlikely to need the ellipsis; you can just cut in and out of the quoted matter when you need to. But if, for example, I want to quote a run of five sentences, leaving out one, I'd need to mark its absence with an ellipsis; or, I might want to leave a clause or two out of a long sentence, such as this one by Andre Aciman:

> And yet, for all I know, everything could start all over again—my father, my mother, the girl with the perfumed wrist, ... my little boy, myself as a little boy, ... the Rosetta stone within each one of us which no one, not even love or friendship, can unburden, the life we think of each day, the life not lived, and the life half lived, and the life we wish we'd learn to live while we still have time, ... and the life we hope others may live far better than we have, all of it, for all I know, braided on one thread into which is spun something as simple as the desire to be one with the world, to find something instead of nothing, and having found something, never to let go, be it even a stalk of lavender.

PART FOUR

TWENTY-ONE GRAMMAR GAFFES AND HOW TO AVOID THEM

COMMON GRAMMAR PROBLEMS AND THEIR SOLUTIONS

Introduction—just between you and I

I could stop teaching grammar now and dedicate myself to the contemplative life or the salvation of the warming world if I'd earned a dollar each time I'd bumped into these grammatical confusions, gaffes and indelicacies in the newspapers, manuscripts, reports and books I read—some of them, sometimes, in my own sentences. But I haven't, and I can't, so here they are.

These are the … I'm trying not to write *errors*, which might make me sound like a member of the club of cardigan-wearing grammar nazis I described in my prologue, but what the hell: here are the errors that trip me up most commonly in my reading and listening. Here are my answers to the grammar questions I'm most commonly asked, to the errors and confusions I most commonly encounter. Here they are, along with some fair-minded discussion of why these slip-ups happen and why it would be better (for you and for the language) if they did not; and here's how to fix them—or avoid them in the first place.

I should add that very good writers break many of these rules for literary effect. But they tend to know the rules before they break them, which makes all the difference. One might fuse or splice a dozen sentences and drop every apostrophe to affect the state of mind of one's character. Dangling modifiers and loose pronoun references, however, rarely help. And unless you're making art, breaking any of these rules is going to look like an oversight, not a device.

Some of these issues I've talked about already (*which* and *that*; *who* and *whom*; the misuse of the *semicolon*, for instance); I'll refer you in those cases. Most of them I've alluded to; some of them I've kept up my sleeve. I'm making this list because, don't tell anyone, but I think there may be some readers who'll start the book here (and maybe stop). Sometimes one needs the answer fast; when your computer crashes and you're on deadline, you may not have time for the chapter and the verse. This is where I troubleshoot; this is the helpdesk. But don't call me if your problem's not on the list. It'll be in the book. Make some time and take it slow and look for it there.

1

Working as an escort in a documentary— dangling modifiers

> Never refresh vegetables that you aren't going to eat immediately under water as it takes away the flavour.
>
> We make recommendations for fixing all the problems in this report.
>
> Denise Hewitt, a so-called friend of Heather Mills, claimed that she worked as an escort with Mills in a documentary that aired on Tuesday night.
>
> The committee agreed to a proposal for a report on the year-to-date status of breaches to be provided to each audit committee meeting.
>
> Situated just two hours south of Sydney or north of Canberra, the experience of visiting Kangaroo Valley is inspiring.
>
> Before she'd even finished laying, Lucy chased the hen out of the coop.

In each of these sentences, a modifying clause or phrase is out of place, suggesting a meaning the writer didn't intend: each has a dangling modifier. In *The Little Red Writing Book*, I confessed to one of my own: *I saw an eastern quoll last night, looking out my kitchen window.*

Thoughts wander when we write. It's easy to sever a modifying expression from the noun it modifies and stick it, inadvertently, before or after a noun it does not. A dangling modifier is a phrase (or a clause) out of place, as a weed is a plant out of place, making a mess of the garden. Most of these sentences fail in other small ways, too, but here they are with their modifiers disendangled.

> Never refresh *under water* vegetables you don't eat immediately ...
>
> In this report, we make recommendations for fixing all these problems.
>
> *In a documentary that aired on Tuesday night*, Denise Hewitt, a so-called friend of Heather Mills, claimed that she worked as an escort with Mills.
>
> The committee agreed to a proposal for the CFO to present, each meeting, a report on the year-to-date status of all breaches.
>
> The experience of visiting Kangaroo Valley, *just two hours south of Sydney or north of Canberra*, is inspiring.
>
> *Before the hen had even finished laying*, Lucy chased her out of the coop.

Here's another I just encountered; I need to give you the first sentence to set it up.

> Enjoy the unique views from ... 25 metres above the ground in the rainforest canopy. *Back on solid ground*, the Escarpment Fly's Café offers a range of food and refreshments.

The writer means *when you arrive back on solid ground, you'll find a range of food and refreshments in the café*. As it stands, it implies that the café has been up in the canopy.

2

She said she had stolen her seashells—loose pronoun reference

A reader, very sensibly, will imagine that a pronoun refers to the last noun mentioned. Make sure it does. Otherwise it gets tricky. It's hard to say for sure who was trying to stop whom in this sentence from this morning's newspaper:

> A successful Hong Kong architect fell nineteen floors to his death with a friend as *he* tried to stop *him* committing suicide.

As he tried to stop him probably means 'the architect tried to stop his friend', but according to the logic that the pronoun refers to the last mentioned (relevant) noun, it might mean 'as his friend tried to stop the architect'. I think it meant the former, but I can't be sure. What about:

> Trying to stop a friend committing suicide, a successful Hong Kong architect fell, with his friend, nineteen floors to his death.

> A successful Hong Kong architect, Nicky Chan, fell nineteen floors to his death with a friend Chan had been trying to dissuade from suicide.

Here's another confusing one. And I'm sorry that it, too, is about suicide. They aren't always.

> The jury heard that the man accused of attacking Ms Hillard, John W Howarth, had written a suicide note and attempted to take his life just hours after she was brutally bashed and left for dead in the garage of her North Sydney home.

This time the pronouns are in the right order, but it becomes hard to follow—one wonders for a second who *she* is, when the pronoun appears in the sentence, so far removed from the woman it alludes to. It would work better if the woman's name were repeated. A bit of reordering would also help:

> The jury heard that John W Howarth, the man accused of attacking Ms Hillard, had written a suicide note and attempted to take his life just hours after Ms Hillard was brutally bashed and left for dead in the garage of her North Sydney home.

Don't be afraid to repeat the relevant noun if it's going to make things clearer. Often, as with the architect and his friend, one needs to rearrange the parts or remake the sentence to avoid the ambiguous connection.

Instead of:

> The boys took all the track from the box and cleaned it. (Cleaned the *box* or the *track*?)

Try:

> The boys took all the track from the box and cleaned the box/the track; or, The boys took from the box all the track and cleaned it; or, The boys took all the track from the box. Then they cleaned the track and put it back in the box.

Instead of:

> George pulled a book from his pocket and read from it. (From his *pocket*?)

Try:

> George pulled from his pocket a book and read from it.

Instead of:

> I took the hat from the pew and set it upon my head. (Set *the pew* on my head?)

Try:

> I took the hat from the pew, and I set the hat upon my head.

Instead of:

> Sarah found a jacket in the wardrobe that her grandfather had worn. (Her grandfather had worn *a wardrobe*?)

Try:

> In the wardrobe Sarah found a jacket that her grandfather had worn. (*Sarah found a jacket that her grandfather had worn in the wardrobe* creates another problem—a dangler.)

Instead of:

> A strong corporate governance regime should help a company identify and stamp out unethical behaviour. This is a key element of any company's success. (*Unethical behaviour* is the key to success? *Stamping it out* is the key? Or *A governance regime* is the key?)

Try:

> A strong corporate governance regime is central to a company's success; it helps a company identify and stamp out unethical behaviour.

If you have two women (or girls) in a sentence, *she* is going to cause confusion:

> Sarah found a jacket in the wardrobe that her grandmother had worn when she was a baby.

Apart from the problem of the wardrobe, which we attended to, had grandma worn the jacket when Sarah was a baby or when grandma was a baby?

One has the same problem with two or more men (or boys):

> Martin told Roger, the departmental deputy secretary, that he had rewritten the report to accommodate the suggestions of his boss. 'He made me do it', he said.

Stop and ask yourself whether each pronoun takes your reader back to the noun you had in mind. If there's room for doubt, straighten the sentence out. Replace some pronouns with the noun they refer to or rewrite the thing completely:

> Martin told Roger, the departmental deputy secretary, that he, Martin, had rewritten the report to accommodate the suggestions of Bob Coombs, Martin's boss [unless he meant *Roger's* boss, the departmental *secretary*]. 'Bob made me do it,' Martin said.

3

Where have all the commas gone— and, while we're at it, the hyphens? Put commas back where they belong

Commas help readers hear what you mean. Too many writers leave too many out. And they put the few they do use in most of the wrong places (more on that in the next two sections).

To remind yourself where commas (and other marks of punctuation) belong, reread Part Three. Commas articulate the structure of a sentence; they keep its key pieces apart for long enough to let you hear the thought the way the writer heard it in his head. Here are some sentences in need of commas. Reading them comma-free, it's hard not to be thrown for a moment, or even genuinely puzzled.

> Our lives are not lived like experiments. If they were scientists would observe and measure the parts ...
>
> We note on the basis of the information there is no material impact.
>
> If your sponsored employment stops your sponsor must advise the immigration department.
>
> However it appears that as this report was generated from old data the problem is easily explained.

> For each parcel of land existing and future needs in regard to local open space … are considered.

They go better like this:

> Our lives are not lived like experiments. If they were, scientists would observe and measure the parts …
>
> We note [that], on the basis of the information, there is no material impact.
>
> If your sponsored employment stops, your sponsor must advise the immigration department.
>
> However, it appears that, as this report was generated from old data, the problem is easily explained.
>
> For each parcel of land, existing and future needs in regard to local open space … are considered.

Most of these sentences could still do with some work; but with commas in their places, one can make sense of them at least.

If you don't articulate the rests in your sentences—the pauses one takes, in speech, between some phrases and clauses—you can't expect your readers to hear them. We forget our commas because we forget our readers. Putting commas in the right places comes with sounding out one's sentences to make sure one's readers can hear the silences as well as the words. For the words can't do all the work on their own—they don't in speech; how could they, on paper?

Hyphens help readers decipher sentences, too; they compound two words, among many, that are meant to be read as one. We're getting out of practice with hyphens. Some deft hyphens might have kept these sentences from implying something they didn't mean; they might have made them clear.

> Her life was uneventful until the sinister life altering illness struck. (*sinister life*? Try *life-altering*)

We apply a risk based audit approach. (*Risk-based* would help)

We outline the process most commonly used to secure long stay temporary entry in America. (Try *long-stay*)

4

Starting a walk with a limp—put a comma after *however*, where you mean *but* (or use *but*)

Always use a comma after *however*, where you use it at the start of a sentence to mean *but*. Otherwise, it sounds like you're using *however* as an adverb (as in *however I look at this*).

The book was longer and later than expected. However it was better.

Try:

The book was longer and later than expected. However, it was better.

Or:

The book was longer and later than expected. It was, however, better.

Or:

Although the book was longer and later than expected, it was better.

A good teacher told me thirty years ago that starting a sentence with *however* is like starting a walk with a limp. *However* works more elegantly mid-clause—after the subject, after the verb, or even at the end of the clause. In the example above, either *It was, however, better* or *It was better, however* would be better than the original. Best of all might be *But it was better.*

However, if you do choose to start with a limp, put a comma after it.

Where you use *however* to start the second of two main clauses in a sentence, favour a semicolon ahead of it (to mark the start of the second main clause) and a comma after it. Don't, in other words, do this:

> We are not expected to discover illicit drug use, however our medical examinations are so complete they are likely to discover any illicit drugs in the athlete's body.

Try, instead:

> We are not expected to discover illicit drug use; however, our medical examinations are so complete they are likely to discover any illicit drugs in the athlete's body.

Or:

> Although we are not expected to discover illicit drug use, our medical examinations are so complete they are likely to discover any illicit drugs in the athlete's body.

But why are we so addicted to this kind of structure? Here's an example from a fundraising letter that just landed on my desk:

> The government provides limited funding, however each year we also rely on fundraising events to 'keep afloat'.

The apologetic quotation marks, the oblique 'limited' and the dreaded *however* opening the second main clause, with no comma after it—all these betray anxiety; they hit a note of strained, uncomfortable and discomfiting formality. Why not this?

> Although the government provides some funding, we need to run fundraising events each year to keep afloat.

Wean yourself off the opening *however*. Subordinate the opening clause (with *although* or something like it), and make a clean start of things in the main clause. Or make the sentence a compound, starting the second with *and* or *but*.

Less formality; more care.

5

They all, ran wild— random and errant commas

I commented in Part Three that the problem is less the demise of the comma than its misuse. I hold to this, despite the evidence of the last couple of entries. I commonly see commas where they don't belong and where, in particular, they don't help. (It often happens when one's subject grows too long, and the best solution is to shorten the subject phrase and drop the comma.)

> One of the qualities that sets her writing apart from the ordinary, is the vivid portrayal of her characters.
>
> (The comma creates two fragments. Trim it, and drop the comma: *One quality that sets her writing apart is the vivid portrayal of her characters.*)
>
> Some of these issues, I've talked about already. (I wrote that in the first draft of the intro to this part. I suppose I did it because that sentence inverts usual word order, beginning with its object. Still, no comma required.)
>
> All three hundred people employed at the Brisbane plant, will lose their jobs when the plant relocates to Thailand next year. (Lose the comma.)

6

Commuted sentences—comma splices, fused sentences and sentence fragments

I talked about comma splices under 'compound sentences' in Part One. Although many good writers break this rule, you don't join two sentences with a comma. Use a full stop or a semicolon or a dash—pieces of punctuation designed for the purpose. Or write *and* after the comma, and make the sentence an honest compound.

A comma alone does not have what it takes to hold two independent clauses—that is, two sentences—apart. To use a comma thus is to commit a comma splice.

> I apologise for the delayed reply, I drafted responses to all your queries yesterday but got distracted by some emergencies in the office.
>
> My friend has a terminal illness, she told me about it ten years ago.
>
> Most of my friends are dedicated to doing nothing much and having it all, it doesn't occur to them they might owe somebody some kind of debt for their good fortune.

You can get away with a comma between main clauses when there are three of them (or more). Where this is the case, you have a series (of clauses); you replace *and* between the first two clauses with a comma; between the last two, you use a comma and *and*. Like this:

> We outgrew the city, we moved to the country, and we're never going to leave.

But don't write this:

> We outgrew the city, we moved to the country, we're never going to leave.

You could write it this way, though:

We outgrew the city; we moved to the country; we're never going to leave.

By contrast, a *fused sentence* runs two (or more) sentences together without punctuation between them. It fuses two independent clauses without a full stop (and cap), an *and* (plus a comma), a semicolon or a dash to keep them apart.

The rain fell for two weeks straight it loosened the gumtrees' grip on the ground when the storm came at the end of all that rain the trees fell.

This is a writer's grammar it is a book about grammar for writers by a writer.

Good, maybe, for literary effect; bad for report writing and a grammar book. Except in artistic hands, fused sentences look like mistakes. No one, at work, means to fuse sentences, but I see them more often than my clients would like me to admit to you. Check for them when you edit. They happen when you write too fast.

A *comma splice* is two sentences falsely linked; a *fused sentence* is two sentences collapsed into one; and a *sentence fragment* is something *less* than a sentence, pretending to be one—punctuated with a full stop. Like:

Good, maybe, for literary effect.

Bad for report writing and, perhaps, your career.

If you're not careful.

Because they look sloppy.

Fragments have their place in good writing. They're good for emphasis. Don't overdo them, though—they look careless. See what I say about them in *The Little Red Writing Book* and in Parts One and Three of this book.

7

There's too many subjects here— if your subject is plural, your verb must be, too

It makes perfect sense when you hear it as a proposition: if you have more than one thing performing the action, the verb must take its plural form; if there's only one actor, the action needs to be expressed in the singular. But it's easy to mess it up in practice.

Watch for four kinds of error.

A *THUNDER AND LIGHTNING'S VERY VERY FRIGHTENING—* TWO SUBJECTS; SINGULAR VERB

'In recent years, alcohol and subsequent liver damage has taken its toll', I heard them say one night on the news, after the death of the great Irish footballer, George Best. Although they were referring to a process, beginning in drink and ending in disease, they used two items (the noun *alcohol* and the noun phrase *subsequent liver damage*) to express it. That amounts to a plural subject. So the verb should have been *have taken* (and the ensuing pronoun should have been *their*):

> In recent years, alcohol abuse and subsequent liver damage have taken their toll.

This error happens all the time. It sometimes occurs, as it did here, because the second part of the subject is a word in the singular, and it comes to mind to write the verb that follows straight after it in the singular. That mistake is forgivable in speech but not on paper. Here are another few examples:

> Mayhem and mass murder *happens* daily in Baghdad. (Verb should be *happen*.)
>
> The huge swell and driving rain *has caused* the abandonment of ferry services till further notice. (*Have caused*.)

Funding and developing Australian Art *is* the business of the Arts Council. (*Are*.)

The obstinacy and corruption of the ruling junta *is* delaying the arrival of aid. (*Are*.)

B *A FLOCK OF GEESE; A RANGE OF OPTIONS*—COLLECTIVE NOUN FOLLOWED BY PLURAL NOUN IN PREPOSITION PHRASE, OR LONG PHRASE OR CLAUSE BETWEEN THE SUBJECT AND ITS VERB

It's easy to be thrown by words intervening between the subject and its verb. When a plural noun is part of a word cluster following the sentence's subject and its verb, a writer will be tempted to make the verb plural. But this defies logic.

Existing and future *needs* in regard to local open space, specifically assessing population projections, demographics and proximity to other public spaces *is considered*. (*Needs is considered*? Plural noun demands a plural verb: *are considered*.)

A range of mountains run along the coast. (Should be *runs*.)

A team of champions *lose* to a champion team every time. (Should be *loses*.)

A flock of geese *take off* from the lake. (Should be *takes off*.)

The bittersweet flavour of youth—its joys, its trials, its wounds, its adventures—*are not* soon forgotten. (Should be *is* not soon *forgotten*.)

Some cases are line-ball. Grammatically, the following sentence wants a singular verb form (because the ensuing words are cast as phrase), even though in real life the sentence describes more than one person doing something. Either the plural or singular is acceptable; but it might be better to recast the sentence.

The CEO, together with her senior managers, *proposes* a new strategy for the organisation. (Could be *propose*.)

The singular verb form sounds more natural if you put the parenthetic expression first:

> Together with her senior managers, the CEO proposes a new strategy for the organisation.

Alternatively, write it this way:

> The CEO and her senior managers propose a new strategy for the organisation.

C THERE'S HUNDREDS OF THEM—THERE IS OR THERE ARE?

People commonly use *there's* or *there is* whether they're talking about something singular or plural to follow. (*There*, in this structure is called the *existential there*, just as *it* in *It is freezing in here* or *It is recommended*, is called the *ambient it*. Both are strange but common usages.) *There* can take either *is* or *are*, and it should take *are* if the noun phrase following (which is its complement) is *plural*. So make it

> There are hundreds of them.
>
> There are seven horses in the yard and a hundred reasons to keep them there.
>
> There are four errors in this equation.
>
> There is only one thing to do.

D NEITHER OF US ARE COMING; NONE OF US CARE

These pronouns point to individuals within a group; each of them requires the singular form of the verb after it: *each*, *either*, *neither*, *everyone*, *everybody*, *no one*, *nobody*, *someone*, *somebody*.

> Each of these pronouns calls for the singular form of the verb.
>
> Neither girl is winning the prize.

Everyone is coming around to the same view.

No one worries enough about this.

Someone is coming.

Traditionally *none* has belonged on that list, and many writers and editors (including me) like the sound of sentences like *none of us is coming*. But Fowler long ago thought it was okay to distinguish between *none of the rain is falling* and *none of the clouds are carrying rain*. I had always followed *none* with *is* on the ground that *none* was a corruption of *not one*—a kind of negative *one*. In my mind it seemed the same kind of word as *no one* or *nobody*, meaning *not a single one among many*. And that still feels right to me; as long as *neither* and *no one* are on this list, I think I might keep *none* on it, too. But I won't insist upon it, because most of the authorities are against me. So take your pick, but don't get precious about it:

None of us wants to see you unhappy.

None of us care what form the verb takes.

8

A hundred words or fewer— the difference between *less* and *fewer*

Nouns of number (plurals, in other words, of *count nouns*) take the determiner *fewer*. If you can write *many*, you write *fewer*:

fewer children, fewer items, fewer books, fewer biscuits, fewer dollars, twenty-five words or fewer.

Nouns of quantity (*non-count nouns*, aka *mass nouns*), because they are singular entities, take the determiner *less*:

Less violence, less volume, less literature, less food, less money.

But *less* commonly gets used with all nouns, count and non-count.

less policies, less children, less items (twelve items or less), less books, less reasons (all these are incorrect)

less water, less time, less hassle, less sense, less leadership (all these are correct)

The distinction still holds. Don't use *less* for all your nouns. If you're talking about a mass of a thing or an indivisible idea or concept—then *less* is the go. If you're talking about a number of things—if you could sensibly put a cardinal number in front of it (twelve items, three children, five books, but NOT five water, and NOT twelve violence), write *fewer*.

9

Peter admires us both; he admires her and me; just between you and me— the case of compound pronouns

Personal pronouns change their form when they become the object of a sentence.

I admire Peter.

Peter admires *me*.

This rule continues to hold, sensibly enough, when you happen to use two pronouns, like *she and I* or a noun and a pronoun, like *Barry and she*, together (as a compound). So, even though many people say (and some people write) something else, the pronouns in compounds like those must change their form when they become the object of the verb (or of a preposition):

Peter has written to Barry and *her.*

The new law works against *us*; it works against *him* and *me.*

This is a lucky break for *you and me.*

Come with me; come with her; come with *her* and *me.*

Just between *us*; just between *us* two, just between *you* and *me.*

10

Whom should I see about this?— when it should be *who* and when it should be *whom*

Who is a pronoun, sometimes interrogative, sometimes relative. In a question, it stands in for a person whose identity is unknown. When it's relative, it refers back to a person just mentioned. In both cases, in the manner of the personal pronouns, *who* changes its form—it becomes *whom*—when it is the object of the clause it opens.

In the question

Whom should I see about this?

I is the subject of the clause (we know that because that's the way you spell that pronoun when it's the subject); *should see* is the verb phrase; *whom* is the object. What the speaker means is—I want to see *someone*, but I don't know who that person is. *Whom* (the interrogative pronoun) is in the form it takes in the accusative case; it is the object of the verb. It takes the form *whom*, not *who*—just as *he* would become *him* in this:

I should see him.

In a relative clause, the pronoun similarly changes form, depending on its role in that clause.

> Marcia Brady, whom I used to love when I was a boy, has gone on to a successful career singing Country and Western.
>
> The judge who was the author of the report said later that his life had been changed by what he discovered when he put the report together.
>
> Graham Greene, whom many people see as the greatest writer never to have won the Nobel Prize, didn't write a bad book. Anyone who can cope with Greene's misanthropic worldview can learn to write by reading Greene's books.

Here's a tricky usage, though, from yesterday's newspaper:

> An alleged stand-over scheme at a Kings Cross strip club involving two burly brothers and another man nicknamed 'fat boy', whom police say is a member of a large cocaine ring …

That *whom* should be *who*—if we write the relevant part of that sentence another way, it becomes clear that *who* is really the subject of a clause: *who is a member of a large cocaine ring, police say.* The word *who* is subject, in other words, of the verb *is*. The clause *who is a member* … is part of the predicate of the clause *police say [that] who/he is a member of a cocaine ring*. The predicate starts at *who*, but *who* is not the object of the verb *say*; all the words *who is a member of a cocaine ring* are, together, the object of that verb; within them, *who* is the subject of the verb *is*.

I told you it was tricky. But the paper, sadly, got it wrong.

11

Please write to myself— the misuses of the reflexive pronoun

There is a reflexive pronoun for each of the personal pronouns:

I	myself
you	yourself

he himself

she herself

it itself

we ourselves

you yourselves

they themselves

one oneself

I described the uses of the reflexive pronoun in Part Two.

He cut *himself* with the knife. (The same pronoun performs and receives the verb.)

She wrote herself a note. (The same person performs and receives the verb.)

They fixed themselves some dinner. (The same person performs and receives the verb.)

I, myself, think it's a terrible poem. (Emphasis)

Daniel wanted to do it himself. (Emphasis)

You don't need the reflexive pronoun for the object of a verb (unless the same person is the subject, too). Many people employ the reflexive when all that's called for is the personal pronoun in its ordinary form:

Please write to *myself* if you have any further questions. (Make it *Please write to me.*)

Herself and myself are looking into the matter. (Just *She and I are looking.*)

These usages express an awkward formality, and they betray an anxiety. Most people fall into the *myself* trap in work or formal settings, where they seem to feel *I* and *me* won't do. But there is no context in which *me* in the first case and *she* and *I* in the second—or any of the normal personal pronoun forms—would not be correct. Keep reflexives for the purposes they were meant for, and don't be embarrassed about *me*.

12

'The his'er problem'—gendered pronouns

Pronouns stand in quite often for singular nouns and for certain pronouns (distributive and indefinite).

> Maree chases the dog; *she* chases *it* all the way down to the river.
>
> The dog chases *its* tail.
>
> *I* love my desk; my friend made *it* for *me*.
>
> *Each* of us needed to make *his* own way.
>
> *Someone* didn't take off *his* boots when *he* walked in from the yard.

When one uses a personal pronoun in the third person singular (*she*, *he* or *it*), a gender issue arises. So, in the sentence where Maree chased a dog, I used *she* for *Maree*, because *Maree*, manifestly, is a woman, and *she* is the feminine form of the pronoun. The gender of the pronoun is uncontroversial in that case. And most nouns have no gender in English; nouns like *desk*, *tree*, *phone*, *sky*, *car*, *journal* and *team* take the neuter pronoun *it*. A few nouns in English are unambiguously gendered: *father*, *mother*, *woman*, *man*, *boy*, *girl*, *daughter*, *son*, *aunt*, *uncle*, *brother*, *sister*—but *not* cousin—and a few more; so it's easy to know which pronoun to use for them.

But what about *the dog*, and what about *my friend*? Many people use the masculine or feminine form (*he* or *she*) for domestic animals if they know the animal or can tell its gender. And if I mean my friend *Henryk*, then I'd call him *he*; I'd call her *she*, if I meant Phillipa. Nor, again, is there a problem with men's and women's names (*Annie* becomes *she*; *Edward* becomes *he*; *Sam* becomes either, depending). But some pronouns—

each, *everyone*, *somebody*—nominate individual people within a crowd that could be made of men and women; and some nouns name a role or station that could be performed by a boy or a girl, a man or a woman; this is where the problem comes. There are many such words. Here are some: *warrior, doctor*, *baby*, *child*, *adult*, *comedian*, *singer*, *critic*, *politician*, *poet*, *cook*, *manager*, *secretary*, *teacher*, *nurse*, *pilot*, *boilermaker*, *priest*, *midwife, cheer-leader* and so on. If I want to substitute a pronoun for such a word—*Every boilermaker must own* her *own tools*—I'm going to have to choose *he* or *she*.

> If a writer wants to write memoir, she's going to lose some friends.
>
> Each manager is responsible for his own staff and budgets.
>
> A pilot must know her own mind.
>
> Everyone must bring his own wine.
>
> To each his own.

That sort of thing …

When one refers to a specific person by means of such a noun, of course, the gender of that person might determine the gender of the pronoun: if I'm writing about the cook in my kitchen now, I could aptly call her *she*. But one should not presume that a word like *cook* is always a *she* or that *chef* is always a *he*.

Where one means all manner of babies or nurses or politicians or executives, whichever pronoun one chooses—because it must be singular and because it can't be neuter—one excludes and offends up to half of the group one refers to. Traditionally, writers resolved the problem paternalistically: one always wrote *he*. These days we recognise the presumption in that solution. And it's a very long time since it was either correct or acceptable.

The same issue arises with words like *chairman*, *batsman* and *policeman*, which have gender written into them, but which in fact, these days, refer to roles or jobs that men and women perform. One should avoid such nouns, except perhaps where you are clearly referring to a male person. One might change the *man* suffix to *woman* where the word concerns a woman (*policewoman* and *businesswoman* sound better somehow than *batswoman* and *chairwoman*, but it may just take some time); or one might change it to the neutral *person*. But, whereas *chairperson*, *salesperson* and *businessperson* almost sound alright, *policeperson* and *batsperson* do not. Or, one might change the noun to *chair*, *batter*, or *officer*. But you're still left with the pronoun problem.

In the examples I listed earlier, the noun in question wasn't expressly gendered and the role it referred to wasn't exclusively male or female. Since it's presumptuous, offensive and often, these days, inaccurate to write *he* unthinkingly after such nouns, what are your options?

A CHOOSE *THEY*

Offend traditional grammar (ians) by using the plural form of the third person personal pronoun (*they*), which is not gender-specific:

> If a writer wants to write memoir, they're going to lose some friends.
>
> Everyone must bring their own wine.
>
> To each their own.

This has been acceptable for a long time.

B GO PLURAL

Alternatively, you can stay grammatical and also avoid gender presumption by making the head noun plural, too:

> If writers want to write memoir, they're going to lose some friends.
>
> All guests must bring their own wine; bring your own wine.
>
> To all their own.

It's nearly always possible to rewrite a sentence this way. But in a very sensitive and subtle essay on gendered language, 'The His'er Problem', Anne Fadiman notes that sometimes, the thing you're getting at loses some critical specificity in the plural. *Every writer worth his salt* is one example she uses. *All writers worth their salt* misses out, she says, 'that fleeting moment in which a reader conjures up an individual writer (Isaiah Berlin in one mind's eye, Robert James Waller in another) instead of a faceless throng.' And *to all their own*, I agree with her, is 'lumpish'.

Her argument is not, by the way, that we shouldn't solve the gender problem, but that solving it comes at a small cost—a loss of umph or grace. Subtle solutions are what we need, not programmatic ones.

C HE/SHE; S/HE; HE OR SHE

Some writers favour substituting for the offensive *he* one of these inoffensive but clumsy constructions:

> If a writer wants to write memoir, he/she is going to lose some of his/her friends.
>
> Everyone must bring his or her own wine.
>
> To each his or her own.

This is, without question, the worst solution. It has the least grace; it's very uncool. Especially bad are the unpronounceable constructs (*he/she* and *s/he*). Is one meant to mouth 'he slash she' or 'he-she'? Don't go this way.

D ALTERNATE *HE* AND *SHE*

You may have noticed that I use this approach. I'll write *Sooner or later a writer will offend most of her friends*; then I'll write *A good cook makes it up as he goes along* the next time I get to write such a sentence. This is another imperfect solution. Some people don't like it much, I know.

But it's not the only thing I try. And this is the point—there's no single solution. Sometimes I go plural; sometimes I try to avoid the structure that causes the issue in the first place. I'd resist *each to his own* and *every writer worth her salt* as clichés anyway. And instead of *If a writer wants to write memoir*, I might write:

> If you want to write memoir, be prepared to lose some friends.

13

We're going on a which *hunt*— which versus that

For my discussion of these two relative pronouns and when one is better than the other, see my discussion under 'subordinate clauses' in Part One (pp 71–9).

I think there are good reasons for keeping *which* for nonrestrictive relative clauses and using *that* for restrictive relative clauses:

> There are just three things [*that*] you need to know.
>
> Determiners are the words *that* occupy the first position in some noun phrases.
>
> Daniel, who arrived in October 2004, is our second child.
>
> Flopsy, Mopsy and Cotton-tail, who were good little bunnies, went down the lane to gather blackberries. (Beatrix Potter)
>
> I'm pleased to enclose two copies of the contract for your book, which we are proud to publish next year.

I believe it makes things easier for writers and better for their sentences to use *that* for definitive modifying clauses and *which* (with a comma before it) to introduce more descriptive, additional, information.

In the end, if you follow this rule, you'll only use *which* when it feels right to put a comma in front of it (when, in other words, you're making a nonrestrictive relative clause). When a comma seems wrong, favour *that*.

You'll find plenty of examples in Part One, but this one demonstrates the choice nicely.

Although one is allowed to write

> The Central West was the only area in the State which got any rain today,

it makes no sense to put a comma in:

> The Central West was the only area in the State, which got any rain today.

That would be to imply that the Central West was the only area in the State—and that it received any rain. This is meaningless.

So, you've got a restrictive relative clause on your hands: leave the comma out, and use *that* instead of which:

> The Central West was the only area in the State that got any rain today.

Word will love you; the squiggly green line will disappear.

What I've described and what I recommend is mainstream American practice; it's also what Microsoft Word wants. In this case, at least, neither of those facts should count against what is, I think, the most robust, clear-eyed and elegant approach.

But most authorities these days, outside North America, adopt a much looser and therefore, I think, less helpful approach than this. And there is plenty of worthy precedent for the use of *which* with restrictive clauses: Shakespeare did it; most writers do; and Fowler allowed it.

So you may, if you like, write:

> The Central West was the only area in the State which got any rain today.

This is the response which the terrorists wanted.

This is the house which Jack built.

Though I would prefer *that* in each of those sentences—Word, I notice, wants it too—*which* is not wrong. Nor is one's meaning any different either way. (Beware, though; as I showed in Part One, sometimes the choice of pronoun alters the meaning entirely.) So please yourself. If you want to get Word off your back, though, use *that* for each of those and for every restrictive relative clause:

The Central West was the only area in the State that got any rain today.

This is the response that the terrorists wanted.

This is the house that Jack built.

Use *which* in sentences more like these:

This track, which passes through steep and dangerous terrain, is not recommended for children.

And now for lunch, which is why you all came here.

The wind, which had now backed to the south, was blowing at gale force.

14

It's a possessive, isn't it? It's or its?

It's means it is. *Its* is a possessive form of the third person personal pronoun.

It's about time we fixed this problem.

It's a matter of opinion.

The storm had lost its sting by midnight.

The carpet-snake wound its body tight around the possum and squeezed the life out of it.

The party elected its new leader.

In my experience, it's one thing to know the difference; it's another to get it right each time you use it. Think hard about what you mean by the sound *its*:

The government issued its new policy.

It's the new policy of the government.

15

Thomas's apostrophes—not every noun that ends in *s* drops the *s* that normally follows the apostrophe in the possessive

Nouns in their possessive (genitive) form look like this:

Mark's, book's, publisher's, desk's, policy's, leader's, tree's, land's, men's, women's, James's, Thomas's.

We add to their tail an apostrophe—and we add an *s*.
For many nouns (like *nouns*) that end in an *s*- or *z*-sound, including most plurals, one may drop the *s* that normally accompanies the apostrophe:

parents', grocers', Pam Peters', poems', banks', books', countries', horses'.

We drop the extra *s* where we don't say it; and we don't say it—mostly with plurals—because it's not easy to say. Hence the exception to the rule. Most of the exceptions, you'll notice, are plurals.

It doesn't follow, though, that every word that ends in an *s* is made possessive by an apostrophe alone. It's a question of what one says. One says *Thomas's* but one doesn't say *horses's* or *parents's*. You write what you say. Here are some words ending in *s* or an *s*-sound that conventionally do take the *apostrophe plus s*:

> Lopez's, Bruce's, James's, Charles's, Thomas's, horse's, mouse's, response's.

Many of these, you notice, are names. It still seems to be a general rule that the names of people, places and institutions (whether or not they end in *s*) want both an apostrophe and a final *s*. Not in church and suburb names, though: *St Marys*, *Kings Cross*, *Frenchs Forest*, *Wisemans Ferry*.

The apostrophe doesn't happen until the noun that's doing the owning has ended. Watch out for

> St Jame's
>
> countrie's.

And you never use an apostrophe for plurals, so none of these can be right:

> Suppliers' of quality beef
>
> Purveyor's of fine coffee
>
> Potato's for sale
>
> He is the author of five book's
>
> Two sonata's in the Italian style
>
> 60's music
>
> JPG's.

16

Dodging bullets—don't use semicolons (or any other piece of punctuation) between bullet points; don't use semicolons to introduce bullet point lists

See what I say under 'semicolons' and 'colons' in Part Three (p 158) to find out why you don't need semicolons between items and bullet point lists.

Not:

For this recipe you'll need:
- one egg;
- two cups of butter;
- one kilo of flour; and
- a bottle of beer.

Nor:

For this recipe you'll need;
- one egg,
- two cups of butter,
- one kilo of flour, and
- a bottle of beer.

But:

For this recipe you'll need
- one egg
- two cups of butter
- one kilo of flour
- a bottle of beer.

And watch out for this kind of thing:

First you will see; Hampden Bridge, opened in May 1898.

17

She's meaner than I; he knows more than I; she likes him more than me

You're meant to write *more than I*, not *more than me*. *Than* is a conjunction, not a preposition; it introduces a subordinate clause of comparison. If it were a preposition, the pronoun or noun following it would be its object (thus, *than me*). But it is not a preposition; hence, *than I*, not *than me*.

> He knows more than I know.
>
> She likes him more than she likes me.
>
> She likes him more than I do.
>
> I am taller than you are (tall).
>
> She knows more about grammar than any other writer knows (about grammar).

When we don't say or write the phrase that follows the subject of that comparative clause, grammar takes it as read:

> He knows more than I.
>
> She likes him more than I.
>
> I'm taller than you [are].
>
> She knows more about grammar than any other writer.

She likes him more than me might be taken to mean that she likes him more than I do, but it should be read as she likes him more than she likes me.

Beware of ambiguities like that or, worse still, this:

> I like Heaney more than Murray. (I like Heaney more than I like Murray, or more than Murray likes Heaney?)
>
> She loves her dog more than her boyfriend. (She loves her dog more

than she loves her boyfriend, or she loves her dog more than her boyfriend loves her dog?)

18

And in the beginning—You may begin a sentence with *And*, *But* or *Because*

Because is a (subordinating) conjunction; it links a subordinate clause or phrase to a main clause. Sometimes the subordinate clause comes second:

> The race meeting was cancelled because of the horse flu epidemic.
>
> Safari can't open the page 'Snorkel # 7' because your computer is not connected to the internet.

Sometimes it comes first:

> Because of the horse flu epidemic, the race meeting was cancelled.
>
> Because your computer is not connected to the internet, Safari can't open the page 'Snorkel # 7'.

Either way is good; either way is grammatical. Why would it not be? The grammar is identical; the meanings are identical, too—though the emphasis differs. It follows that you may start a sentence with because.

If, on the other hand *because* is all your sentence says, you've written a fragment. *Why do you need the car keys?* Your father asks you. And all you say is *Because*. It won't get you the car keys and it won't make a valid sentence. Similarly, *Because I want them*, is a fragment, and therefore ungrammatical.

But there's nothing wrong with *because*, itself—not at the start of a sentence (as long as it is soundly made); not anywhere.

And and *but* are conjunctions, too. They coordinate rather than subordinate. Sometimes what they coordinate are two main clauses. And sometimes those two clauses appear as two separate sentences. When that's the case, *and* or *but* are good for the work of joining them. You may, in other words, begin a sentence with *and* or *but*. The *Bible* does it; Virginia Woolf does it; judges do it; journalists do it; grammar has always allowed you to do it. Just don't overdo it. That's the real rule. But then, that's the rule for just about everything.

19

Up with which I will not put; to boldly go—end with prepositions; split your infinitives

It's now perfectly permissible as a matter of usage, and it always has been okay grammatically, to end a sentence with a preposition (*This is something we won't put up with*) and to put an adverb in the middle of an infinitive verb form (*to absolutely forbid*; *to deeply regret*).

See page 61 of *The Little Red Writing Book*.

20

Brian's conducting was the eighth wonder of the world—possessive form of the pronoun before a gerund

A word like *conducting*, as I just used it, is a present participle serving as a noun. It's a noun, like *moustache* in *Brian's moustache*, and Brian owns it. So Brian needs an apostrophe; the noun before a gerund (or verbal) in this kind of construction is possessive. So:

> Brian's conducting was the eighth wonder of the world.

On the other hand, you might leave the apostrophe out if you wrote about a similar set of circumstances a little differently:

> I went along just to see Brian conducting.

You could read *conducting* in that sentence as a *gerundive*, modifying the noun *Brian*. Then again, you might put the apostrophe back in this case,

> I went to the opera for the joy of watching Brian's conducting,

where *conducting* seems to be a noun again; it's the conducting you go to see, not Brian. The difference is the same as that between these two sentences:

> They sat and read Ernest's writing.
>
> They sat and watched Ernest writing.

The second is in the same league as *The first thing he saw was Mr McGregor hoeing onions.* Peter saw Mr McGregor, who was, it happens, hoeing; the fans watched Ernest, who was, it happens, writing.

So, when the lawyer signs off his letter, saying

> We appreciate you taking the time to assist us with this,

though he's trying to be nice, he is at once ungrammatical and stuffy. What he meant was:

> We appreciate your taking the time to help us with this. OR
>
> Thanks for helping us with this.

Where the present participle is working as a noun (where it's a *gerund*), write the noun or pronoun ahead of it (*your* ahead of *taking*, in my last example) in its possessive form; where the participle is a modifier (a *gerund*) leave the noun or pronoun in its habitual form.

Do you have a problem with *my* writing this novel during my lunchbreak?

My *son's* swimming made me very proud.

The chances of *your* finishing on time are only slim.

But:

I watched my *son* swimming up and down the pool like a world champion.

She wanted, before she died, to watch Brian conducting the Berlin Philharmonic.

21

'I think he said, "I'll come tomorrow"'—It's okay to switch tense, but not by mistake

Although it is often said one shouldn't switch tense in a sentence or a paragraph, what is meant is that one shouldn't switch tense without meaning to, or without meaning anything by it. So it looks bad to write:

We were walking down to the dock and when we get there we've stood for two hours and look out at the sea.

I arrive here today and I found a complete mess.

We find that the company had very high levels of stress ... We found that the company has very high levels of staff turnover.

Choose a ruling tense for your narrative, whatever it is. Use it consistently, and don't switch out of it accidentally.

But there are many reasons why, within a sentence or a paragraph, a writer may change tense. They're illustrated by the sentence in my subheading:

> I think he said, 'I'll come tomorrow'.

The writer or character thinks now that someone else said yesterday, using the future tense at that time, 'I'll come tomorrow'. Three tenses in one sentence, all quite legitimate.

I *hope*, in the present tense, that my friend BB will win the contract on Tuesday (in the future tense). It follows that anytime I *recommend* a course of action—to my children, to my students, to the agency under review—I recommend it for the future, even if it is the near future. (*We recommend that the government begin, in its first term, a 'root and branch' review of the taxation system.*) In this case, though, the verb *begin* is not in the future tense; it's in the subjunctive mood.

One may write, by the way, either that one *finds* or that one *found* certain things to be true. Neither is more correct than the other. *Finds* is the verb in its plain present tense; *found*, in its plain past. Each tense works. To write *found* doesn't imply that the finding no longer holds; to write *finds* doesn't imply that one is only just this second (and for this second) making that finding. Choose one tense for making your findings and keep using it. It's only when you're inconsistent that readers start wondering if it's you or they who've lost the plot.

Consistency, as ever, is the trick. Beyond that, work out exactly what you're trying to say and say it, using all the tenses you need.

Note these perfectly everyday and orthodox sentences in which the tense changes at least once:

> Because I have read a million books, I am getting better at guessing the kind I will like.
>
> If you're thinking too hard about impressing the selectors, you will almost certainly fail.
>
> I imagine you will have forgotten all about me by the time you have left the front gate.

EPILOGUE

LEARN THE RULES; FORGET THE RULES

I

Good writers know their grammar—so well, in the end, they stop thinking about it and get it more or less right most of the time. This is what Basho meant when he wrote: 'Learn the rules; forget the rules'. There's simply too much to know to keep it all in your head. This book may have shown you that. But I hope it's also shown how important it is to keep asking questions about how you're using words and forming sentences. Practise: this is also what Basho meant. Observe the disciplines as well as you can, failing quite often, and having to look them up all over again (in this book or another); over time, many of the virtuous habits of the grammatical writer will become second nature. What will certainly become second nature is the habit of thinking of your sentences as structures—structures that invent and carry meaning into the world. Keep thinking of your sentences, then, as physical structures: this is what writers do; this is their practice. Keep asking yourself how sound and smooth your sentences are, how well made, how well scored. Keep asking questions.

Like a car on a wet night, a car in the hands of a driver who's had a drink or two more than they should, a sentence will get away from you if you don't know some things about phrases and clauses (main and subordinate), sentences (compound and complex) and where in the hell to stick the punctuation. But hear how powerful this one is, precisely because it strains at its syntax without snapping it—hear how fit it is for describing this particular moment.

> My daughter is walking along the roadside late at night—too late, really, for a seventeen-year-old to be out alone even in a town as safe as this—and it is raining, the first rain of the season, the streets slick with a fine immiscible glaze of water and petrochemicals so that even a driver in full possession of her faculties, a driver who hasn't consumed two apple martinis and three glasses of Hitching Post pinot noir before she gets behind the wheel of the car, will have trouble keeping the thing off

> the sidewalk and out of the gutters, the shrubbery, the highway median, for Christ's sake... But that's not what I want to talk about, or not yet, anyway.
>
> —TC Boyle

These sentences, on the other hand, are less masterful. Their grammar fails them, or they push hard against the rules to no good effect, or their punctuation is errant, and they sound, at best, awkward, and, at worst, barely comprehensible.

1 With only 21 thoughtfully appointed rooms, bridal parties and their guests are charmed by the intimate ambience of the house, sumptuous furnishings, elegant architecture and peaceful gardens with sweeping views of the Highlands.

2 For each parcel of land existing and future needs in regard to local open space, specifically assessing population projections, demographics and proximity to other public spaces is considered.

3 Enjoy the unique views from the edge of the Escarpement amongst the rainforest canopy, 25 metres above the ground. Back on solid ground, the cafe offers a range of food, refreshments and snacks and the opportunity to browse our range of gifts and souvenirs or simply relax in our visitor centre.

Between these two positions—brilliant writing that plays the grammatical lines, and sloppy writing that misses all the lines and hits the net every time—lie paragraphs like the one that follows. It's not flashy; nor is it sloppy. It's just competent and clear (if, by necessity, bland). It deals with material that's hard to be clear, let alone vivid, about; imagine how much harder it would be to follow if the grammar got in the way.

> Tax expenditures have no generally agreed definition. In practice, what constitutes a tax expenditure can change over time and between jurisdictions. In Australia, the Taxation Expenditures Statement 2006 (TES 2006) defines a tax expenditure as

> *a tax concession that provides a benefit to a specified activity or class of taxpayer*

> Unlike claims on outlay programs, claims on tax expenditures lie outside of the direct control of government officials. Under the tax self-assessment arrangements, taxpayers effectively use tax expenditures to 'write their own cheques', whereas government officials must 'write the cheques' for financial assistance provided through outlays. As a consequence, the effectiveness of numerous tax expenditures can often only be ascertained after the fact—through ATO audits of taxpayers, for instance.

II

Grammar—the structure of the language as we use it—is mathematical. It's logical, but it's not pedantic. One needn't—indeed, one can't, really—choose between correctness and expressiveness. Getting your grammar right shouldn't stop you being lucid or lyrical or imaginative at the keyboard; it's what linguistic accomplishment depends on.

Grammar's a constraint, but it's not an encumbrance. It constrains the act of creating meaning with words—beautiful meaning, if the writing is art; unambiguous meaning, if the writing's more functional. The better you master your grammar, the more your words say. If writing is painting, grammar is the edge of the canvas; it's the rules of the competition; it's the deadline. If writing is sport, grammar is the rules of the game. Go ahead and play like Roger Federer, if you can learn, like him, (barely) to clear the net and (barely) to keep the ball in court at impossible speeds and angles. By all means play the lines; but play by the rules, or it's simply not tennis you're playing, and the skills you manifest are no longer beautiful or meaningful.

Every artist—the cellist, the watercolourist, the haiku poet, the dancer—has to find a way to transcend, but not to ignore, the limits of their medium. To master them; not to be mastered by them. Without cheating. For the writer, grammar is the limits.

If grammar constrains a writer, it's the kind of constraint that frees. The rules of grammar are the rules for paradise. Writing is the paradise.

REFERENCES

Booher, Dianna 1988, *Good Grief, Good Grammar*, Ballantine, New York.

Colman, Ruth 2005, *The Briefest English Grammar Ever!*, UNSW Press, Sydney.

Dykes, Barbara 1992, *Grammar Made Easy*, Hale & Iremonger, Sydney.

Fadiman, Anne 1998, *Confessions of a Common Reader*, Farrar, Straus, and Giroux, New York.

Fowler, H Ramsey and Aaron, Jane E 2006, *The Little, Brown Handbook* 10e, Longman, New York.

Gowers, Ernest et al. 1987, *The Complete Plain Words*, Penguin, London.

Hale, Constance 1999, *Sin & Syntax*, Broadway Books, New York.

Huddleston, Rodney and Pullum, Geoffrey 2002, *The Cambridge Grammar of the English Language*, Cambridge University Press, Cambridge.

—— 2005, *A Student's Introduction to English Grammar*, Cambridge University Press, Cambridge.

Hughes, Barrie et al. (eds) 1993, *The Penguin Working Words*, Penguin, Ringwood.

Kane, Thomas 2000, *The Oxford Essential Guide to Writing*, Berkley Books, New York.

Murray-Smith, Stephen 1987, *Right Words*, Viking, Ringwood.

O'Conner, Patricia T 1996, *Woe Is I*, Putnam, New York.

Partridge, Eric and Whitcut, Janet 1999, *Usage and Abusage* 3e, Penguin, London.

Peters, Pam 2007, *The Cambridge Australian English Style Guide*, Cambridge University Press, Cambridge.

Purchase, Shirley 1998, *The Little Book of Style,* Department of Finance & Administration, Canberra.

Siegal, Allan & Connolly, William 1999, *The New York Times Manual of Style and Usage*, Random House, New York.

Shaw, Harry 1994, *Errors in English and Ways to Correct Them*, HarperCollins, New York.

Snooks & Co 2002, *Style Manual for Authors, Editors and Printers* 6e, John Wiley, Milton.

Trask, R L 1997, *The Penguin Guide to Punctuation*, Penguin, London.

—— 2000, *The Penguin Dictionary of English Grammar*, Penguin, London.

Tredinnick, Mark 2006, *The Little Red Writing Book*, UNSW Press, Sydney.

University of Chicago Press Staff 2003, *The Chicago Manual of Style* 15e, University of Chicago Press, Chicago.

Weiner, E S C and Delahunty, Andrew 1993, *The Oxford Guide to English Usage* 2e, Oxford University Press, Oxford.

Dictionaries

Butterfield, Jeremy et al. (eds) 2003, *Collins Australian Dictionary* 5e, HarperCollins. Glasgow.

Deldridge, A et al. (eds) 1997, *The Macquarie Dictionary* 3e, The Macquarie Library, Macquarie University, Sydney.

Pickett, Joseph P, et al. (eds) 2000, *The American Heritage Dictionary of the English Language* 4e, Houghton Mifflin, Boston.

Authors quoted

Alexie, Sherman 1993, 'This Is What it Means to Say Phoenix, Arizona', *The Lone Ranger & Tonto Fistfight in Heaven*, Grove/Atlantic, New York.

Allen, Pamela 2004, *Cuthbert's Babies*, Penguin, Ringwood.

Antrim, Donald 2003, 'I Bought a Bed' in Fadiman, Anne (ed), *Best American Essays 2003*, Houghton Mifflin, Boston.

Auden, W H 1976, 'In Memory of W. B. Yeats' (1939) *Collected Poems*, Faber & Faber, London.

Basho, Matsuo 2000 *Knapsack Notebook* (1687), in Hamill, Sam (ed. and trans), *Narrow Road to the Interior & Other Writings*, Shambhala, San Francisco.

Boyle, T C 2005, 'Chicxulub', *Tooth & Claw*, Viking, New York.

Chandler, Raymond 1943, *The High Window*, Penguin, Harmondsworth.

Chaucer, Geoffrey 1990, *The Canterbury Tales* (c1390) Phoenix, London.

Davidson, Robyn 2006, *No Fixed Address*, Quarterly Essay Issue 24, Black Inc, Melbourne.

DiCamillo, Kate 2004, *The Tale of Despereaux*, Walker Books, London.
—— 2007, *Great Joy*, Candlewick, Cambridge, Massachusetts.
Dickinson, Emily 2000, 'Poem XXXII', *The Selected Poems of Emily Dickinson*, Modern Library, New York.
Di Lampedusa, Giuseppe Tomasi 1960, *The Leopard*, William Collins, London.
Fadiman, Anne 1998, 'The His'er Problem', *Ex Libris*, Farrar, Straus, and Giroux, New York.
Frazier, Charles 1997, *Cold Mountain*, Atlantic Monthly, New York.
Frost, Robert 1973, 'Stopping By Woods' (1923), *Selected Poems*, Penguin, London
'Genesis', *The Bible*.
Groff, Lauren 2008, 'Lucky Chow Fun', in Henderson, Bill (ed) 2008, *Pushcart Prize XXXII*, Puschart Press, New York.
Hemingway, Ernest 2007, 'The Art of Fiction' (1958) in Plimpton, George, *The Paris Review Interviews Volume I*, Canongate, Edinburgh.
Hest, Amy & Jeram, Anita 2003, *You Can Do It, Sam*, Candlewick, Cambridge, Massachussetts.
Lopez, Barry 2008, 'Emancipation', unpublished.
Malouf, David 2006, *Every Move You Make*, Chatto & Windus, Sydney (p 80).
Margulis, Lynne & Schwartz, Karlene V 1998, *Five Kingdoms* 3e, Freeman, New York.
Matthiessen, Peter 2003, *The Snow Leopard* (1978), Vintage, New York.
Maxwell, William 1998, 'Nearing Ninety', in Ozick, Cynthia (ed), *Best American Essays 1998*, Houghton Mifflin, Boston.
McCarthy, Cormac 1985, *Blood Meridian*, Random House, New York.
Melville, Herman 2000, *Moby-Dick* (1851), The Modern Library, New York.
Muth, Jon J 2003, *Stone Soup*, Scholastic, New York.
Oliver, Mary 2004, 'Flow', in *Long Life*, Da Capo, New York.
Plimpton, George 2007, *The Paris Review Interviews Volume I*, Canongate, Edinburgh (from 'Ernest Hemingway, The Art of Fiction').
Pope, Alexander 1711, 'An Essay on Criticism'.
Potter, Beatrix 1902, *The Tale of Peter Rabbit*, Frederick Warne, London.
Shakespeare, William 1597 *Richard III*.
—— 1597, *Romeo & Juliet*.
—— c1603, *Macbeth*.
—— 1608, *King Lear*.
Sorkin, Aaron 2000, 'Trip 9s', scene one, episode 2, 'Mr. Willis of Ohio', Season One, *The West Wing*.
Spragg, Mark 2004, *An Unfinished Life*, Knopf, New York.

Stegner, Wallace 1971, *Angle of Repose*, Doubleday, New York.
Tolkien, J R R 1937, *The Hobbit*, George Allen & Unwin, London.
Tredinnick, Mark 2007, 'Eclogues', *Eclogues*, Hunter Writers Centre, Newcastle.
—— forthcoming in 2009, *The Blue Plateau*, UQP, St Lucia.
Twain, Mark 1901, 'Corn-Pone Opinions'.

ACKNOWLEDGMENTS

For a long time this book seemed beyond me—there was always so much grammar and so little time. And then, once I'd begun, there was so little space. For waiting, I thank my publisher Phillipa McGuinness; for doing just about everything else at home, while I did this, I thank Maree, who won't ever stop inspiring me.

Too many shelves in my shed are groaning with grammars and slouching with style guides; I mention in my references the best of these books—the ones I leaned on most heavily—and I thank all of them here. You don't have to know everything, you see; you just have to know where to look; and it helps if that's not far from your desk. But, to be honest, most of my grammar, such as it is, I got from reading stories and poems, plays and memoirs by people who'd mastered it first, who'd learned the rules and forgotten them beautifully—or whose editors made it look that way. Thanks to the writers, then, some of whom I quote from here; thanks for the books that keep the language new. Now it's our turn.

If there's one task more exacting than writing a book on grammar, it's editing it; Edward Caruso, my editor, pulled that off with grace and efficiency. He even noticed my jokes. Even grammar can laugh. Thank you, Edward. I am grateful to UNSW Press for supporting *The Little Red Writing Book* and for taking on this one. At the press, I thank, in particular (and in addition to my wonderful and patient publisher, Phillipa—see above), Joanne Anderton, Heather Cam, Lauren Crozier, Chantal Gibbs, Uthpala Gunethilake, Di Quick, Rosie Marson, Ella Roby, the marketing team, Jane Kembrey and Unireps. Many thanks to Geoff Whyte for his intense, forensic reading of the first printing of the book. His close and careful reading prompted this revision, which picks up a number of typographic, stylistic and spelling errors that escaped my notice in the first printing, and which only go to show how easy it is to fall short of one's own standards of care. Geoff, in my experience, never does. So, thanks. Thanks to Chantal Gibbs, too, for her hard work on the revision.

For a decade or so I've run grammar programs at universities and writers' centres and inhouse for clients. For supporting those programs, thanks to Anne-Maree Britton at the ACT Writers Centre; to Arabella Lee, Anne-Marie Nolan and Ambra Sancin at the NSW Writers' Centre; to Jennifer Dustmann, Lisa Elias, Jo Fleming, Brett Myers, Liselle Pullen, Jan Sayer and Danielle Williams at the University of Sydney's Centre for Continuing Education; to Michelle Willoughby at the Australian Catholic University; and to Lesley Nelson at Collaborative Business.

And thanks to my students over the years; I'm about ready to teach you something now.

INDEX

–*ed* verb form 93, 97
–*es* suffix 174
–*s* verb form 92
–*s's* possessives 175

a 22, 51–2, *see also* indefinite articles
abbreviations
  a or *an* before 53
  acronyms 53, 177–8
  capitalisation of 112
  contractions 134, 17
  full stops in 134
abstract nouns 41–2, 111–12
abstract verbs 42
acronyms 53, 177–8
active voice 90
adjectival phrases 31, 45, 56, 64–5
adjectival verbs (gerundives) 32, 45, 59, 95, 233
adjectives 43–4
  compound adjectives 45, 64, 168–9
  pronouns as 120
  punctuating lists of 138
  verbs used as 94
adjuncts 46
adverbial conjunctions 140, 156–7
adverbial phrases 56, 64
adverbs 46
  compound adverbs 64, 168
  punctuating lists of 138
ambient *it* 214
an 52–3, *see also* indefinite articles
and 140–2, 212–13, 232, *see also* conjunctions
angle brackets 195
animals 220
apostrophes 173–8
  common errors in use 227–8
  of possession 110–1, 115, 175
appositives 27
  noun phrases as 63–4
  nouns as 109
  punctuating 139
articles 22, 51–3, 113, 125, *see also* determiners
aspect 100, 106
attributive adjectives 44
Australian style
  abbreviations in 134
  direct speech 147
  hyphens in 165
  relative clauses 73–4, 76–7
  series comma 136–7
  that vs. *which* 73–4, 76–7
  'youse' 118
auxiliary verbs 99–102, 106

Basho 16, 239
because 231
being words, *see* verbs
braces 195
brackets 180, 192–3
British style
quotation marks 185
series comma 136–7
bullet points 151–2, 158–9, 229
but 140–2, 207–8, 231–2, *see also* conjunctions

Canada, misplaced comma makes news in 149
canonical clauses 64–7
capitalisation after quotation marks 188–9
cardinal numbers 126
carrier sentences 186, 189–91
case
of nouns 114–15
of pronouns 120
catenative construction 60–1, 102
Chicago Manual of Style, *see* US style
clauses 13, 54–6
canonical 64–7
defined 55, 64
pronouns standing for 43
punctuating strings of 138
closed questions 39
closing parentheses 194–5
collective nouns 113, 213–14
colons 150–3, 161, 190
commas 135–50
after conjunctive adverbs 81
after *however* 207–8
before conjunctions 48, 81
before relative clauses 72
before *which* 224–5
common errors in use 205–6, 209
pauses articulated by 131–2
splicing with 82–3, 210–11
common errors 199–235
common nouns 42, 112–13
commuted sentences 210–11
comparative clauses 79
comparatives 230–1
complements 27
complex catenatives 61
complex intransitive clauses 65
complex sentences 83
complex transitive clauses 66
complex words 162, 167
compound adjectives 45, 64, 168–9
compound adverbs 64, 168
compound–complex sentences 84
compound nouns 45, 109, 169–72
compound pronouns 216–17
compound sentences 80–3, 140–2, 153–7
compound verbs 168
compound words 172–3
concrete nouns 41, 111–12
concrete verbs 42
congealed words 164
conjunctions 48–9
beginning sentences with 231–2
commas and 140–2
nouns and 109
semicolons and 155
conjuncts (conjunctive adverbs) 47, 81–2
content clauses 69, 79
continuous form 107
contractions 134, 173, *see also* abbreviations
convoluted expressions 142–3
coordinating conjunctions 48, 80
count nouns 114
curly brackets 195

dangling clauses 71
dangling modifiers 200–1
dashes 143, 159–62
declarative mode 38–9
declarative sentences 23, 37–40, 65–7
deep structure 19
defining clauses 73
defining pronouns, *see* restrictive relative clauses
definite articles 52–3
definite determiners 126
definitive modifying clauses 224
degrees of quality, expressing 45–7
delayed joining words, commas and

145–6
demonstrative adjectives 121–2, 125
demonstrative pronouns 121–2
dependent clauses 55, 67–79
determinative phrases 126
determiners 51, 125–6, *see also* articles
gendered 220–4
pronouns as 90, 122, 125
dialogue (direct speech) 146–7, 184
direct objects 28–9
direct questions 135
direct speech 146–50, 184
directive sentences 36, 38, 86, *see also* imperative mood
disjuncts 46
distributive pronouns 125
ditransitive clauses 66
ditransitive verbs 96–7
doing words, *see* verbs
double-barrelled names 166
double quotation marks 185–6

each 125–6, 214–15
either 125–6, 214–15
ellipsis 195–6
em-rules 163–4, *see also* dashes
en-rules 163–4
errant commas 209
errors, common 199–235
essential modals 101
everybody/everyone 23, 214–15
ex–, hyphen after 167
exclamation marks 180–2
exclamations, commas after 145
exclamative mode 38–40
existential *there* 214

Fadiman, Anne 223
families of tense forms, *see* tense
fewer vs. *less* 215–16
find/found 235
finite verbs 20–1
first person pronouns 117
five verb forms 91–6
formality 15–16
forms, *see* tense
four sentence structures 79–86
fragments, *see* sentence fragments
freight train (run-on) sentences 80–1, 138, 141
full stops (full points) 131, 133–5, 186
functional grammar 26–34
functions of verbs 91
fused sentences 210–11
future tense, *see* tense

gender
common problems in use of 220–4
in third person pronouns 116, 119, 124
genitive, *see* possessive forms
geographical units 112, 178
German word order 35
gerundives (adjectival verbs) 32, 45, 59, 95, 233
gerunds 59–60, 95, 232–4
grammar
common errors 199–235
defined 11–16
rules of 239–42
'grocers apostrophe' 174, *see also* apostrophes

h–, *a* or *an* before 53
he 118–19
he/she/it/they choice 220–4
helper verbs, *see* auxiliary verbs
horticulture, quotation marks in 185
however 47, 207–9
Huddleston, Rodney 13
on canonical clauses 64–7
on catenative constructions 61
on comparative clauses 78
on indirect objects 30
on supplements 58
on verb phrases 61
hyphens 162–73, 206–7

I (pronoun) 117, *see also* personal pronouns
imperative mood 23–4, 35–6, 37, 39
indefinite articles 22, 52–3, *see also* articles

indefinite determiners 126
indefinite pronouns 123–4
independent clauses 55–6
    punctuating 140–2, 152, 155–6
    sentences as 21, 25
indicative mood 23, 37, 105
indirect objects 28–9
indirect questions 135
infinites 60–1
infinitive phrases 33, 55, 60–1
infinitives, splitting 232
informality 15–16
interrogative mode 38, 179–80
interrogative pronouns 122–3
interruptions, punctuating 161, 195–6
intransitive clauses 65–6
intransitive verbs 96–7
introductions, commas after 139–40
inverted commas, *see* quotation marks
irregular plurals 177–8
irregular verbs 98–9
its/it's 226–7
italics, quotes and 184

Latin, case in 114
legal language 149–50
less vs. fewer 215–16
lists, *see also* bullet points
    colons and 150–3
    punctuating 229
    semicolons in 157–9
    serial commas 136–9
loose pronouns 202–5

marginal modals 101–2
mass nouns 113–14, 215–16
meaning, grammar makes possible 11
missing words, commas standing for 146
modalities 100
modal auxiliaries 101–2
modern grammar 13–14
modifiers 26, 43
    articles as 52
    dangling 200–1
    phrases as 50, 57
    role in sentences 30–1
    subordinate clauses as 67
    verbs as 91
modifying clauses 33
modifying compounds 166
mood 37–40, 91, 100, 103–5
myself 219–20, *see also* personal pronouns

Nadal, Rafael 34
names, *see also* nouns; proper nouns; titles
    apostrophes omitted from possessive 228
    double-barrelled, hyphenating 166
    gendered 220–1
neither 125, 214–15
nobody/no one/none 125, 214–15
non-count (mass) nouns 114, 215–16
none 214–5
nonfinite verbal phrases and clauses 62, 144
nonfinite verbs 20–1, 94–5, *see also* verbals
nonrestrictive relative clauses 73, 76, 143–5
noun clauses 68
noun phrases 57, 62–4, 147–8
nouns 41–2, 108–15, *see also* pronouns
    articles used with 51–2
    as gerunds 59–60
    as primary parts of speech 89–90
    collective nouns 113, 213–14
    compound nouns 45, 109, 169–73
    functioning as adjectives 45
    gendered 220–4
    possessive form 174
    punctuating series of 136–8
number (plurality)
    gendered pronouns and 222
    irregularity in 176–7
    of nouns 109–10
    of verbs 91
    subject–verb agreement and 212–15
    verb forms 99
numbers
    as adjectives 44
    as determiners 126
    cardinal numbers 126

pluralising 177–8

object complements, noun phrases as 63
objects 26
belong with verb 148
noun phrases as 63
nouns as 109
phrases as 57
pronouns as 216–17
role in sentences 28–30
one/oneself (pronoun) 118, 121, 123–4, *see also* personal pronouns
open questions 39
ordinary intransitive clauses 65
ordinary transitive clauses 66

paratactic form 81, 82, 153–7
parentheses 160–1, 193–5
parenthetic expressions
commas in 142–3
dashes enclosing 160–1
punctuating 192–5
parts of speech 12–13, 40–53
passive voice 24–5, 28, 34, 90
past participles 59, 93–5, 97–8
past tense, *see* tense
pauses, punctuating 131–2, 135
perfect continuous form 108
perfect form 107
periods (full stops) 131, 133–5, 186
person, of pronouns 117
personal pronouns 44, 117–9
common errors in use 216–24, 230–1
Peters, Pam
advocates modern grammar 13
on abbreviations 134
on catenative construction 61–2
on commas 135, 137, 140
on compound nouns 169
on hyphens 165
on irregular verbs 98
on marginal modals 101–2
on phrasal verbs 51
on subjunctive mood 104
on *that* vs. *which* 74
phrasal verbs 51, 58
phrases 13, 54–6
defined 54
pronouns standing for 43
types of 56–64
plain verb form 91–2
plu-perfect form 107, *see also* tense
plurality, *see* number (plurality)
possessive adjectives 125
possessive forms
apostrophes in 173–4, 227–8
before gerunds 232–4
its/it's 226–7
of nouns 110–11
of pronouns 115–16, 120–1
post-nominal adjectives 44
postmodern poetry 193
predeterminers 126
predicates 19, 22–5
prefixes, hyphens and 162, 167
prenominal adjectives, *see* attributive adjectives
prepositional phrases 23, 50–1, 57–8
indirect objects as 30
role in sentences 57
subject–verb agreement and 213–14
prepositions 49–50, 109, 232
present participles 59, 95, 107, 232–4
present tense, *see* tense
primary auxiliary verbs 100
primary parts of speech 43, 89–90
pronouns 42–3, 115–25
ambiguity in 202–5
as adjectives 44
as primary parts of speech 89–90
common errors in use 216–24
compound pronouns 216–17
gendered 220–4
possessive form before gerunds 232–4
reflexive 121, 218–20
relative, in subordinate clauses 70–8
subject–verb agreement and 214–15
proper nouns 42, 112–13, 166, 178
punctuation 13, 129–96, *see also* commas

quantitative adjectives 126
question marks 179–80

questions 36–7, 39, 135
quotation marks 146–7, 182–91
quoted text 152–3, 184–5, 196

random commas 209
references, punctuating 153
reflexives 121, 218–20
regular verbs 97–8
relative clauses 70–8
relative pronouns 43, 67, 70–8, 122–3
restrictive relative clauses 24, 32, 72
    commas and 143–5
    that vs. *which* 73–6, 225
round brackets (parentheses) 160–1, 193–5
rules of grammar 239–42
run-on sentences 81, 138, 141

's, *see* apostrophes
salutations, commas after 145
schools of grammar 13
second person pronouns 118
secondary parts of speech, *see* modifiers
Seinfeld on exclamation marks 181
semicolons 131, 153–9
    before conjunctive adverbs 81
    before *however* 208
    bullet points and 229
sentence fragments 21, 84–6, 161, 210–11, *see also* subordinate clauses
sentences
    as structures 239
    common errors in use 210–11
    complex 83
    compound–complex 84
    compound sentences 80–3, 140–2, 153–7
    four structures of 79–86
    inner life of 19–25
    meaning conveyed by 12–13
    role of punctuation in 131
    simple 79–80
serial commas 136–9
shall 101
she 118–19, see also *he/she/it/they* choice; personal pronouns
should 101
sic 192
simple sentences 79–80
single quotation marks 185–6
singular and plural, *see* number (plurality)
slash brackets 195
'sneer quotes' 183–4
speech acts 38, *see also* direct speech
speechwriting, dashes in 159
split infinitives 232
standard English 16
Style Manual, *see* Australian style
subject complements 33, 63, 109
subjects 19, 20–8
    agreement with verb 212–15
    noun phrases as 63–4
    nouns as 109
    of directive sentences 36
    phrases as 58
subjunctive mood 38, 40
    auxiliary verbs in 100
    tenses vs. 235
    verb forms 103–5
subjuncts 46
subordinate clauses 24, 67–70
    dependency of 21, 67
    in complex sentences 83
    in compound-complex sentences 83–4
    semicolons between 157
subordinating conjunctions 49, 68, 71
suffixes 174, 222
supplements 58
syntax, *see* grammar

taxons 90
technical terms, quote marks in 183–4
tense
    –ed verb form 93
    –s verb form 92
    consistency in use 234–5
    verb forms 21, 90, 105–8
than 230–1
that 121–2
    vs. *which* 73–8, 143–5, 224–6
the 22, 52, *see also* definite articles

The West Wing 129–30
there/there's 214
these 121–2
they 118–19, 124, 222, *see also he/she/it/they* choice
third person pronouns 118–19
  gender in 116, 124
this 121–2
those 121–2
titles 112, 178, *see also* names; proper nouns
to be
  as auxiliary verb 100
  present participles and 95
  verb forms 90, 93–6
to do 100
to have 93–5, 100
topic of a sentence 27–8
traditional grammar 13
transformational–generative grammar 13
transitive clauses 66–7
transitive verbs 96–7

unfinished sentences, punctuating 161, 195–6
US style
  abbreviations 134
  brackets 192
  compound sentences 141–2
  hyphens 165
  past participles 97
  punctuating lists 137
  quotation marks 185–6, 188–9
  subjunctive mood 104
  that vs. *which* 73, 225

verb phrases 42, 58–62
verbals 20–1
verbs 26, 28, 42, *see also* compound verbs
  agreement with subject 212–15
  as primary parts of speech 89–97
  belong with object 148
  compound verbs 168
  finite, in sentences 20–1
  functioning as adjectives 45
  irregular verbs 98–9
  phrases as 58
  regular verbs 97–8
  requiring specific prepositions 50–1
  role in sentences 28
vernacular 15, 58, 118
vocatives 36, 145
voice
  active voice 90
  passive voice 24–5, 28, 34, 90

we 117, *see also* pronouns
well–, hyphen after 169
West Wing, The 129–30
what 122
when 78
where 78
which 122–3
  vs. *that* 73–8, 143–5, 224–6
who/whom/whoever/whomever/whose 72–3, 76, 122–3, 217–18
will (modal) 101
word clusters, *see* clauses; phrases
word order 21, 34–7

you 118, *see also* pronouns

FSC
www.fsc.org
MIX
Papier | Fördert
gute Waldnutzung
FSC® C083411

Zeitfracht Medien GmbH
Ferdinand-Jühlke-Straße 7
99095 Erfurt, Deutschland
produktsicherheit@kolibri360.de